YOU CAN'T

TALK TO ME

THAT WAY!

YOU CAN'T
TALK TO ME
THAT WAY!

Stopping

Toxic Language

In the Workplace

ARTHUR H. BELL, Ph.D.

CAREER
PRESS

Franklin Lakes, NJ

YOU CAN'T TALK TO ME THAT WAY!
EDITED AND TYPESET BY CHRISTOPHER CAROLEI
Cover design by Johnson Design
Printed in the U.S.A. by Book-mart Press

To order this title, please call toll-free 1-800-CAREER-1 (NJ and Canada: 201-848-0310) to order using VISA or MasterCard, or for further information on books from Career Press.

The Career Press, Inc., 3 Tice Road, PO Box 687,
Franklin Lakes, NJ 07417
www.careerpress.com

Library of Congress Cataloging-in-Publication Data

Bell, Arthur H. (Arthur Henry), 1946-
    You can't talk to me that way! : stopping toxic language in the workplace / by Arthur H. Bell.
        p. cm.
    Includes bibliographical references (p.) and index.
    ISBN 1-56414-822-X (paper)
    1. Bullying in the workplace. 2. Language in the workplace.
3. Verbal self-defense. 4. Invective. I. Title.

HF5549.5.E43B45 2005
650.1'3--dc22

                                                                    2005042168

Dedication

To my son Arthur James Bell, with congratulations on his completion of the Ph.D. in Linguistics at Cornell University and his new career at the State Department. Our occasional approaches to verbal conflict over the years almost always ended in laughter.

Acknowledgments

Research interest in verbal abuse in the workplace is in its infancy, with far less investigative or analytic work in its corner than has been done for allied problems such as sexual harassment/abuse and physical violence at work. With recognition to those who have begun such research, my first debt of gratitude goes to the "front line" of more than one hundred executives, managers, supervisors, and rank and file employees who let me in to the sometimes embarrassing, sometimes frightening, and always fascinating world of their own experiences with (and observations of) verbal abuse over the course of their careers.

In particular, I want to thank leaders at Charles Schwab, Price Waterhouse Coopers, PaineWebber, the U.S. Navy, Cisco Systems, Oracle, TRW, Johnson & Johnson, Cost Plus World Market, American Stores, Artex Knitting Mills, the U.S. State Department, Apple Computer, Sun Microsystems, British Telecom, Deutsche Telekom, Santa Fe Railway, Global Technologies, Wells Fargo, the U.S. Coast Guard, Lockheed Martin, and many other companies and organizations small and large. All demonstrate a deep commitment to workplace values and employee relations that leave no room for verbal abuse.

I also thank my colleagues at the University of Southern California, Harvard University, the Naval Postgraduate School, Georgetown University, the University of San Francisco, and elsewhere, for the conversations and contacts that helped shape this book. And once again, for the third time, I express my admiration and gratitude to my editors and production experts at Career Press, most notably Michael Pye, Kirsten Dalley, Christopher Carolei, and Linda Rienecker. Through their tact and patience, we all managed to avoid verbal conflict in the process of producing a book about it.

Finally, I want to thank my friend and agent Grace Freedson for her faith in this project and her hard work on my behalf.

Contents

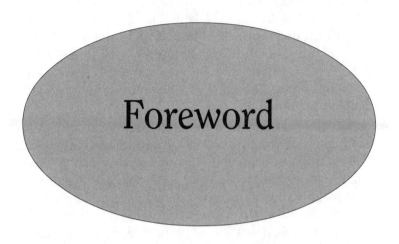

Foreword

The importance of this book lies in its expert, practical advice on what to do about an extremely serious problem in business, government, the military, and other organizations. Abusive language between bosses and subordinates, or between peers, has the immediate result of spoiling relationships (and productivity based on such relationships), and the long-term effect of ruining morale, teamwork, and loyalty.

The plain fact, as Art Bell argues eloquently, is that "you can't talk to me like that" without consequences of some kind. In some situations, the victim of abusive language snaps back, causing an emotional dustup that occupies the attention and energy of the office for hours or days at a time. (Scars from the more spectacular verbal blowups can last for years in some companies.) At other times, the victim clams up and refuses to do his or her best work, or any work at all, after experiencing verbal stings. Perhaps most devastating of all to the workplace is the effect of the rumor mill, which divides workers into armed camps depending upon whose side of the argument they favor. Multimillion dollar projects have come late to market, or have fallen through entirely, based solely on the fact that workers couldn't get along.

Much of management research in the last few decades has been devoted to discovering and understanding the "something else" beyond financial incentives that keep employees striving to do their best. Art Bell has broken new ground here by surfacing a well-known but little discussed antagonist to business processes and employee motivation. His definition of abusive language, his rationale for why it occurs, and his remedies for resolving and preventing it all have the potential to set dysfunctional organizations back on a productive track. The success of most business ventures, after all, depends upon smooth, reliable, and respectful interactions between people. When these bonds break down due to abusive language, the gears of business and industry no longer mesh. Client relationships, business promises, and corporate goals all come crashing to a halt.

Just as valuable as this book's advice to individuals is its program for corporate policies and procedures. Tolerance for abusive language within an organization is a cultural issue, not unlike a company's attitudes and rules regarding sexual harassment, racial discrimination, or age bias. Art Bell shows, with actual training syllabi and sample policy statements, how companies can take a stand against abusive language at all levels within the organization. The fruit of such action, of course, lies not only in its essential morality but also in the very real benefits it pays to the company and its employees. A workforce that does not have to cower in the face of a boss's withering verbal attacks experiences less stress, takes fewer sick days, engages in less litigation over a hostile work environment, and tends to give more effort and exhibit more creativity. Companies are the beneficiaries, in terms of profits, innovation, and employee loyalty, of these feelings of mutual respect and workplace safety.

Few of us have not had occasion to spout off with a blast of colorful language at some point. But Art Bell points out that the business environment is not the place for those verbal eruptions. From legal, strategic, and human relations perspectives, the costs of abusive language in the workplace are far too great compared to any temporary boost such verbal attacks might achieve in "building a fire" under someone. The beauty of this book is that is takes us from what *should* happen in organizations to practical ways in which they *can* happen.

Read this book and take it to heart if you play a leadership role in any kind of organization. Just as important, provide the book to your employees as a highly readable, sensible guide to their use of language in the workplace.

Thomas J. Housel, Ph.D.
Associate Chair and Professor of Information Sciences
Naval Postgraduate School
Monterey, California
May 2005

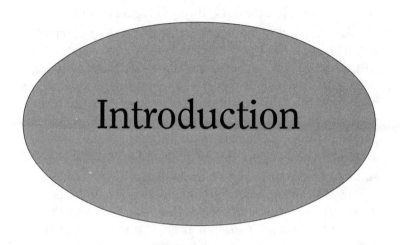

Introduction

The more you know about verbal abuse in the workplace, the more able you will be to stop it or avoid it.

This book lets you look at the problem of verbal abuse through many sets of eyes. You will wince along with victims or "targets" of verbal abuse as they endure rage and insults. Switching hats, you will get inside the heads of a few verbal abusers themselves to learn what makes them tick (like time bombs, unfortunately). You will stand within the arena of verbal abuse as one of the spectators to the trauma; the rest of the workers, after all, witness the brouhaha or hear about it (usually in exaggerated form) via the company grapevine. You will have the opportunity to evaluate your own vulnerability, both as a target for verbal abuse, and perhaps as a perpetrator. You will hear the dramatic story of how verbal abuse impacts companies and individuals in dozens of negative ways. Here you will find complete information about your options within the company and, if necessary, through legal channels.

Above all, you will learn strategic ways to communicate the message, "you can't talk to me like that!" You will discover ways to deal with verbal abuse as it happens, and ways to put the pieces of your professional life back together in the aftermath of an abusive situation, in manners that build better business relationships for the future, without letting the guilty off the hook.

As a business school professor and management consultant, I have the day-to-day challenge and privilege of helping business people (including business students) understand and resolve problems that interfere with the attainment of their professional goals and those of their companies. Frankly, one of hardest issues to discuss in the workplace—for all of us—is the problem of abusive language. We tend to overlook, excuse, or pretend to forget these incidents much in the same way that domestic violence and verbal abuse gets hidden from friends and neighbors. In some cases, we're ashamed to be victims of verbal abuse at work. In other cases, we're furious at our verbal abuser but don't know what to do. In still other situations, we're embarrassed at being singled out for verbal abuse in the presence of our coworkers. Our temptation is just to forget the whole thing.

Until it happens again. And, of course, verbal abuse does reoccur, usually in more and more amplified and vicious ways. A 2005 Gallup poll found that one employee out of six reported feeling so much anger at a coworker that he or she felt like hitting the person. The line between sustained verbal abuse and physical violence is thin indeed. Obviously, verbal abuse, and the anger it arouses within us, can't be closeted or compartmentalized as just "the boss's personality" or "a business fact of life."

This book attempts to put the topic of abusive language squarely before us all—bosses, managers, kingpins, queen bees, and worker bees—so we can think intelligently about the problem, gain insight into our own experiences as victims (and perhaps as perpetrators) of verbal abuse, and, most important, find more productive, less destructive ways of relating to one another at work.

Although I cannot provide individual counseling or specific advice on particular situations at your workplace, I do welcome your feedback, comments, and questions as you read this book. You can reach me at bell.ah@comcast.net. Companies and other organizations interested in policies and programs on abusive language are asked to contact me at the Masagung Graduate School of Management, University of San Francisco, San Francisco, California 941117, email bell.a@sbcglobal.net, tel. 415-435-4245.

Arthur H. Bell, Ph.D.

Belvedere, California

May 2005

Chapter 1

Who Cares About Verbal Abuse?

Books are written with real people and real problems in mind. *You Can't Talk to Me That Way! Stopping Toxic Language In the Workplace* focuses on five groups of readers. There's a good chance you are a member of one or more of these groups.

Verbal Abusers and Their Victims

1. *Those who are the now the targets of verbal abuse in their workplace.* These people suffer regularly, sometimes daily, from a withering barrage of demeaning, insulting language from bosses, coworkers, or clients. They have endured jibes about their race, religion, sexual preference, disability, national origin, accent, gender, marital status, and appearance. Short of quitting their jobs, they want to know *what to do* to stop the hail of language that threatens to destroy their dignity, motivation, productivity, and professional confidence.

2. *Those who manage "big mouth" supervisors and other employees.* Skilled managers know what a black mark it will be for their careers to tolerate verbal abuse on their watch, even when they themselves do not indulge in it. They recognize that verbal abuse can ruin team spirit, cripple individual contributors, and invite expensive litigation. Sheltering verbal abusers among their direct reports inevitably comes back to bite the manager. Quarterly results sag as office life becomes a verbal battleground. Executives upstairs begin to ask what's going on. "Where to hide?" occupies the attention of workers, who should be thinking about what to do and how to win.

3. *Verbal abusers themselves.* This especially applies to those with the tendency to erupt at the slightest provocation, or to store up anger for periodic explosions. These people

are not monsters; in fact, they often have the reputation of being among the most dedicated to the company. Why else would they expend so much emotional energy on business issues? In their view, why else would they care so passionately? Over time, however, they have lost control of their tongues. Even in their best moments, they shade most communications to subordinates with an edge of sarcasm. At their worst, they berate people to their faces and assassinate reputations behind their backs. Many of these verbal abusers want to change their behavior—or have been told by their boss or the company lawyer that they *must* change their ways. They may be turning to this book in an effort to learn what they are doing wrong, how it affects others, and how they can change. They also may be using this book as a text in a company-mandated class on ending verbal abuse.

4. *Friends, spouses, and significant others who want to help victims of verbal abuse or perpetrators of verbal abuse (who are, after all, victims of their own abusive behavior).* It's painful to watch someone you like or love going through daily battles with a verbal abuser. It's equally upsetting to live with or observe a friend or spouse whose language is out of control in the workplace, and probably at home as well. These people may come regularly to their friends and spouses to "vent" about their problems. Throughout the chapters of *You Can't Talk to Me That Way!* friends and relatives can find insights on how to be more than a bystander or good listener in these situations.

5. *Business leaders who want to understand some of the interpersonal forces that keep their organizations from achieving top level results.* Business cultures that have tolerated verbal abuse can best be changed when executive leaders "get the message" and resolve to stop abusive language in its tracks. In some cases, this change begins with the company president or CEO. When this person demonstrates by example that abusive language won't be tolerated, others quickly fall in line. On the flip side, when the leader at the top tears into people, subordinates follow his or her negative example.

What Is Verbal Abuse?

Let's define our terms clearly from the beginning by setting aside what verbal abuse is *not*. Verbal abuse in the workplace is not any communication that hurts your feelings. Bosses, coworkers, subordinates, and clients not only have the right, but often the obligation, to "call a spade a spade" and tell you about the pluses and minuses of your work performance. You may not like what you hear, but those negative feelings alone do not mean you have been verbally abused.

Verbal abuse also cannot be defined as *any* form of heated or angry communication. Workplace stress, including the positive stress of challenging opportunities, inevitably causes feelings of all kinds to surface. A boss may be red in the face with anger when a major contract falls through, and he or she may bluster to all within earshot about his disappointment and exasperation. But this expression of feeling is not in itself an automatic instance of verbal abuse. People have always shown their feelings at work and will continue to do so, including feelings of bitterness and frustration. As a general rule, it can be said that those who care least about their jobs show the least emotion at work. Supervisors should not seek to banish passionate commitment, and the appropriate language of feeling that flows from it, from the workplace.

Finally, verbal abuse cannot be defined solely as swearwords, although such language does often occur in bona fide examples of verbal abuse. The use of such words as *goddamn, son of a bitch, asshole,* and so forth in the workplace may be distasteful to many people—and, in the extreme, can create a hostile work environment that threatens their users continued employment. For people of strong or fundamentalist religious conviction, the use of such language may be offensive on religious or moral grounds. But swear words in themselves are not verbal abuse. A boss who says, in the course of a team briefing, that "the damn regulators in Washington don't understand that we're trying to run a business here" has probably not verbally abused those in the audience, nor would any court take up a complaint based on his occasional salty language. By using such expletives, bosses may damage their image in the eyes of some employees—but they also might enhance their image to those employees looking for a gung ho, swashbuckling leadership style.

Helpful Dictionary Definitions

A quick Google search will demonstrate that the word "abuse" is used exponentially more often in connection with the phrase "sexual abuse" (10 million hits) or "physical abuse" (10 million hits) than with our topic, verbal abuse (1 million hits). Because of that dominant association, the word "abuse" may be colored by connotations of perversity, torture, and emotional gore. Those connotations, while true in the most extreme cases of verbal abuse, are not helpful for mainstream understanding. Let's return, instead, to the Latin roots of the word "abuse" *Ab* means "away from," as in "abnormal" (away from the normal). Verbal abuse, by this definition, is verbal treatment that is "away from" the usual and appropriate "use" to which you are accustomed in the workplace. That departure from the normal state of things can relate to at least six areas:

1. *Tone.* A manager's (or other colleague's) tone can be unusually harsh, sarcastic, angry, or belittling in comparison to the tone he or she typically uses in conversation with you and other employees.

2. *Content.* What's said can contain topics that stray far from what is expected and appropriate in the workplace. Examples would include sexual references, comments about alcohol or drugs, or evaluations of personal grooming and dress.

3. *Language.* The vocabulary used in verbal abuse may be crucially different, especially in the use of foul language, than words used for ordinary business messages.

4. *Nonverbal signals.* The speaker's facial expressions, posture, hand and arm activity, and physical movement

(pacing, for example) all send signals in verbal abuse incidents that differ remarkably from the nonverbal aspects of day-to-day business conversation.

5. *Audience.* Verbal abusers sometimes restrict the audience for their assault strictly to one person—for example, a victim alone in a boss's office. Alternately, verbal abusers sometimes choose to maximize the public embarrassment of their victim by choosing as large an audience as possible—during a meeting, for example—for their verbal onslaught.

6. *Volume.* Verbal abusive messages are, on average, delivered in a louder voice than regular business talk. However, if the volume of the message is reduced to a hiss in the victim's ear, that volume too differs from ordinary practice in business.

Recognizing Verbal Abuse

So what are the key recognition signs of verbal abuse? Few of us mistake the sting of verbal abuse when it is directed at us. We instinctively know when a boss, co-worker, or other person has crossed the line between ordinary criticism (deserved or undeserved) and has begun to use language that *demeans important aspects of who we are.* We know when someone is trying to humiliate us. Our internal "abuse detectors" seldom give false readings.

But with an eye toward stopping verbal abuse, it can be helpful to name and examine the five most common characteristics of verbal abuse in the workplace. Knowing the techniques of the attacker can give us a distinct advantage in developing strategies to thwart those assaults and insults.

1. Verbal abuse focuses on who we are, not what we do. Our behavior in the workplace is fair game for critique and comment, especially in formal or informal performance evaluations. Certainly a boss can legitimately tell us, "You said you would have this report on my desk by noon today and you're already two hours late." That kind of criticism focuses on what we have done (or, in this case, not done). People who don't want their actions to be critiqued probably should avoid business life altogether.

But what if the boss says, "You're a liar! You promised to have this report on my desk by noon today and you haven't followed through. You're just like the rest of your people!" Then the focus of his diatribe is no longer on critiquing our behavior, but instead on denigrating our character and humanness. No one wants his or her race, religion, sexual preference, disability, national origin, gender, marital status, or appearance to become fodder for the abuser's cannon.

2. Verbal abuse focuses on inflicting pain, not on expressing emotion. In meetings, one-on-one interviews and conferences, and "water cooler" or after work conversation, it's not uncommon or particularly disturbing for a boss or coworker to vent his or her feelings about work frustrations. "I just can't believe they beat us to market with that product!" a boss may rage. "We've got to get our goddamn engineering department talking to our marketing people."

This kind of bluster is inward-directed, in the sense that the boss is simply trying to let out feelings of anger over a business failure. Even if a few engineers are present to hear the boss's diatribe, they don't take his words as personal attacks.

However, if the boss steps up to a couple engineers and says, "You faggots in engineering and your goddamn incompetence have cost us this market opportunity!" then the language is clearly outward-directed. The language is no longer focused on venting, but rather honed to injure at a deep level.

3. *Verbal abuse plays on vulnerabilities in a way that discourages constructive change.* We each have areas of our personalities or character that are especially sensitive to insult or criticism. Verbal abusers locate these vulnerabilities, and then prey on them *not* as a means of helping us improve our business attitudes or skills, but instead as a way of making us feel increasingly awful about ourselves and our abilities at work.

Let's say, for example, that Linda (an administrative assistant) is by nature somewhat shy. She tends to blush a bit when she meets new people and isn't particularly good at making instant small talk with strangers in the workplace. Her supervisor, Alice, takes perverse delight in reminding Linda on a daily basis of her lack of confidence around others. Even though Alice speaks softly and at times with a syrupy sweetness to Linda, her communication is nonetheless abusive in intent and in result.

Take last Thursday, for example. Linda, along with other "admins," was scheduled to attend an in-service training session for the afternoon. Alice motioned Linda into her office for her daily dose of verbal poison. "Linda, you're going to embarrass me and our work group if you don't speak up and show some intelligence in this training session," Alice told her. "Being a pussy around here isn't going to get you anywhere. You act like you're afraid of your own shadow. Do you have psychological problems?"

These words from her supervisor cut Linda deep. Her supervisor picked the exact personal characteristics and tendencies that Linda finds most difficult to change. (Last year Alice had taken a similarly abusive approach in her often repeated words to an overweight employee—"Tubby, dear, you'll never look professional until you slim down"— until the persecuted worker took the company to court over the matter and won, much to Alice's chagrin.)

The key to recognizing verbal abuse based on vulnerabilities lay not so much in the exact words used by the abuser as in the apparent malice and repetitive verbal attacks that characterize such assaults. These attacks on an area of personal vulnerability are often masked as teasing or attempts at humor (a gambit Freud called "tendency humor"). For example, a verbally abusive boss publicly uses the term "Gramps" when referring to an older employee who is worried that his age threatens his status and promotability within the company. Or a supervisor tortures a full-figured female employee with regular comments about breast reduction surgery.

In all such cases, a personal characteristic or quality about which the targeted person can do very little (even if he or she chose to) becomes the zone where the abuser turns the knife of cruelly intended comments.

4. *Verbal abuse is out of proportion to any reasonable communication for a given situation.* Sometimes, even when a negative comment or punitive response is justified, the

verbal abuser will "turn up the volume" in relation to the content, emotional intensity, and public visibility of the confrontation.

Consider the example of Nathan, a new salesperson, who inadvertently tallies his monthly sales figures incorrectly. His boss, a petty dictator with a long history in the company of picking on new employees, storms down the hall waving Nathan's monthly report. "This is precisely what I don't want, Nathan," the boss shouts. "You've bumped up your monthly figures to make yourself look better. Any retard can add a column of figures. Do I have to look over your shoulder to make sure you don't fudge the numbers? Is a village around here missing an idiot?"

Under this public onslaught, Nathan withers inside. He admits he made a mistake, but certainly does not think that the boss needs to start World War III over his error. In this case, the boss is cutting butter with an ax.

5. *Verbal abuse is often accompanied by a violent, memorable act or gesture.* Those who practice verbal abuse want their victims to remember their encounter with *The Beast* forever. At the same time, abusers want to stigmatize the victim in the eyes of others. Nothing fits this bill better than a dramatic act or gesture that punctuates and memorializes the abusive language. In the workplace, such an act can be the loud slamming of a door, the tearing up of an employee's paycheck or work product in front of a group, the sending away of an employee from a meeting table, or the breaking of objects (pencils and pens are favorites) and throwing of desk items (staplers and tape dispensers regularly go flying in some offices).

These violent acts say loud and clear to the targeted victim, "I view you as a child I can traumatize. I want to control you by your fear of me," in the same manner an angry, overbearing parent attempts to dominate and terrorize a cowering child. The symbolic act of violence carries the clear message, "I want to hurt you."

Changing Things for the Better

We can all think of things to make our work lives better. The close parking spot, for example, would brighten the day. A corner office with terrific views might also sweeten our work hours. But when asked in surveys what they would like to change about their workplace, many American employees give a somewhat surprising answer: they simply want people to talk to them civilly. Exit interview data across industries makes the same point. The most common reasons employees give for quitting are that they "couldn't get along with their boss" and they "didn't like their coworkers."

These men and women are tired of enduring a workplace where they struggle to take home a semblance of human dignity along with their paycheck each week or month. They are sickened by the thought of getting up each morning to face verbal attacks, tirades, and abuse throughout the business day. They don't like to dodge people at work for fear of their sarcasm and wrath, or to walk on egg shells during meetings and hallway conversations lest they ignite the dynamite of the boss's or a coworker's temper.

Friends who hear about such verbal abuse in the workplace aren't shy about giving their solutions: "Tell that loud mouth to stuff it," "sue the jerk," "transfer out of his division," or "just quit." But those options, appropriate and tempting as they may be in some extreme circumstances, usually don't help the great majority of us who simply want to fix a local instance of verbal abuse as efficiently as possible and get on with our mortgage, our kids' education, and our petunias. In most cases, we aren't eager to start litigation against our employer ezcept as a last resort. We also don't picture ourselves fighting fire with fire by getting into a shouting match with our verbal attackers, nor are most of us financially able on a given day simply to pack up our desks and quit. Besides, we won't let anyone make us quit.

For the long-suffering and often courageous American workers who want to remain at their jobs and solve the problem of verbal abuse, this book has a virtual armory of weapons to use in fighting back and reclaiming a workplace where individual dignity is respected and observed. Key among those weapons is the ability to say, "you can't talk to me like that!" whether in these exact words or something like them.

This book will show you how to:

♦   Recognize verbal abuse—and distinguish it from acceptable criticism, expressions of strong feeling, and honest disagreement.

♦   Understand the verbal abuser. Knowing what makes him or her "tick" helps you prepare a strategy for ending verbal abuse.

♦   Grasp the personal characteristics (or other attributes) that have possibly made you a target for verbal abuse (although such abuse is by no means your fault). If you've been a sitting duck for verbal potshots, this book will find you another seat.

- Find both short-term and long-term solutions to end verbal abuse and restore harmony to working relationships.

Chapter 2

Why Me? Vulnerability Factors for Verbal Abuse

If you are a victim of verbal abuse, you have no doubt looked around your workplace and wondered why others (perhaps those more likely for, and even deserving of, attack in your eyes) had escaped the *Wrath of Khan*. In this section, we investigate personal attributes that may serve as attractors for verbal abuse—but, importantly, we do so *not* to displace the blame for verbal abuse from the abuser to the victim. Instead, we want to understand any factors that increase your vulnerability as a likely prey for a verbal abuser. Socrates urged people to, "Know thyself," in part as an excellent way to prepare for confrontations with others.

Those experiencing physical attack, particularly in cases of rape, often must endure a period of inevitable soul-searching in which they ask, "Was it me? Did I do something to provoke this attack? Am I to blame?" Through the love of friends and the intervention of counselors, these victims generally come to realize that they did no wrong and were, in fact, sinned against rather than the one who committed a sin. But this realization does not preclude some tactical reflection and future strategizing on their part. In other words, a person who has been attacked in a dark alley may ruefully and wisely conclude not to walk alone in dark alleys again. We can learn from painful experiences that were not our fault.

In this light, here are ten "dark alleys," as it were, that often prove to be catalysts or enabling circumstances that help to explain why some are targeted for verbal abuse, rather than the person sitting next to you in the workplace.

1. Your personality style may conflict directly with the style of your abuser. (Note, again, that your right to maintain your own personality is not at issue here. Instead, we are investigating what attributes helped to define you as a target.) As treated in detail in chapter six, personality styles can be broadly described in the categories of the Member, Self, Juggler, Planner, Thinker, Empathizer, Closer, and Researcher. Each of these types, born of both nature and nurture, view life through a

somewhat different window. What one type sees as per-
fectly appropriate and desirable may be seen as totally
obtuse and absurd by another type.

For example, a Thinker likes to find intellectual reasons for what happens at work and in life. When those
reasons prove correct, the Thinker is delighted and con-
gratulates himself on seeing things clearly. When those
reasons prove inadequate in some way, the Thinker is frustrated and goes on to seek better reasons and answers.

By contrast, an Empathizer has less use for reasons
and rationality. The Empathizer wants to experience and
act upon the emotions that accompany decisions and
events. Shall we move our headquarters to Boston? The
Empathizer wants to know how the workforce *feels* about
such a change. The Thinker wants to know whether such
a move makes good business sense. You can easily imagine that Thinkers and Empathizers become involved in
some of workplace's most vociferous arguments. Thinkers see Empathizers as stupid; Empathizers see Thinkers as coldhearted. Those emotional ingredients can easily
be whipped up into an incident of verbal abuse from one
side or the other.

Perhaps a dramatic difference in personality style
helps to explain why a verbal abuser targeted you. As the
prime object of their frustration, you and your way of
seeing the world angered and threatened them. Although
their resulting actions of verbal abuse can't be excused,
simply recognizing the difference in personality types
between you may be a valuable insight as you try to prevent incidents of verbal abuse in the future —and, as is
most often the case, go on to work with someone who
verbally abused you.

For example, you may decide in your next conversation with "the enemy" to recognize up front your mutual

differences in personality style: "Jack, I understand that
you want specific reasons for our decisions in the company—and I recognize the value in that. But I want you
to recognize the value of some of us who are 'people-
persons' in the company. We take the pulse of how employees are feeling about things, what motivates them,
and what doesn't. I think those insights are also valuable. Otherwise we end up with a great, reasonable plan
that no one wants to follow. I'll listen to your perspective if you will listen to mine."

2. Allied to the issue of differences in personality style
is the reality of temperament conflicts. Recent research at
the University of California, Berkeley and elsewhere demonstrates that, as infants, we bring with us into this world
certain behavioral preferences—"trailing clouds of glory,"
as it were. Most notably, some of us are on the shy side
from birth (the "introspective" or "introverted" among
us), and some are outgoing (the "extroverts").

It is not uncommon for introverts to wonder why extroverts are so loud, so unreflective, and such busybodies. At
the same time, extroverts wonder (aloud, of course) why
introverts are so timid, uninvolved, and even antisocial.

These powerful and basic temperament differences,
particularly at times of business stress, can flow over into
verbal abuse. An extroverted boss may lay into an introverted subordinate for not showing more gung ho enthusiasm during a boisterous evening out with important clients.
"Don't you know how to have fun?" the boss might ask.
"Can't you cut loose even for one evening? You made us
look terrible by your hangdog face at the bar."

Just as easily, an introvert boss could turn verbally
abusive to an extrovert subordinate. "Wilson, you acted

like an ape in heat during that sales presentation. What was all that shouting and arm waving? You should have just presented your facts calmly and confidently. You made us all look like jackasses."

The solution to temperament difference, of course, is not to convert the entire workforce to one temperament type or another. Instead, managers and employees at all levels need to be aware of the possible influence temperament differences can exert on their workplace interactions. Having the humility to admit that your temperament isn't the only acceptable temperament starts the process of synergy (making the most of a variety of types and talents) and makes less likely the eruption of verbal abuse between unlike temperament types.

3. You may also be between the crosshairs for receiving verbal abuse if you have intentionally or accidentally positioned yourself as the *point person* for vital business functions or processes. Nixon's famous line comes to mind: "If you can't stand the heat, stay out of the kitchen." Let's say, for example, that your company's financial future depends primarily on the number and quality of innovations coming out of its Research and Development Division—a division you proudly head. Because so much is riding on the positive results of your division's work, the rewards and kudos to you will be substantial if your division turns out stunning new concepts and designs. On the other hand, you may well confront verbal abuse, even from the company's top leaders, if your division fails in its mission.

In this case, your organizational placement helps to account for your vulnerability to verbal abuse much more than your personality or temperament. Although verbal abuse is not the inevitable inheritance of all point people on the organizational chart, they can be advised to be watchful for verbal eruptions when they come and to prepare ways to deal with them. Shakespeare's line remains true for the brightest and best in the company: "Heavy lies the head that wears the crown."

4. You may be perceived as the employee who will bounce back, but not push back. That is, your accepting, patient demeanor and even-headed manner may be taken by the boss or other potential abuser as a "get out of jail free" card when it comes time to shout at someone. Just as family psychologists have located the "symptomatic child" within homes—the lightning rod child who seems to draw down on himself the wrath of the parents in a way that siblings don't—organizational psychologists have identified the punching bag employee. (In the old Three Stooges films, Curly was clearly the punching bag in the trio.) This often pummeled individual is good at hanging his head in the face of a verbal attack from the boss, and then going on with life as if nothing had happened. Meanwhile, the boss has used this punching bag to send a potent message to all other employees who saw or heard about his verbal abuse: "Shape up or this poor schlemiel could be you!"

Playground bullies are notorious for picking upon the child they judge to be least likely to fight back, withhold lunch money, or tattle to the teacher. The climax of many books about growing up features the comeuppance of the bully, as the apparently timid child finds the courage (and ninja sticks, a la Hollywood's *The Karate Kid*) to fight back.

If you feel you have been cast as the bounce back punching bag in your work situation, you can end the verbal abuse that comes your way by striking back—albeit sanely, shrewdly, and strategically—to let your attacker know that you won't take it anymore. Some tools for such a comeback are described in Chapter 10.

5. You may fall prey to verbal abuse because one of your most dominant attributes is drawing the full fire of your abuser. Let's say, for example, that you are the youngest, newest employee in your department. Your manager, several decades older than you, seems bent on making you "pay your dues"—by which he means taking the worst jobs, accepting regular insults, and receiving little or no thanks.

Sadly, the manager may be playing out a revived *Big Me/Little You* scenario that bruised him once upon a time as a young employee. For whatever reason, your youth has put you in the path of verbal abuse. (Note, virtually *any* way in which you differ from your surrounding colleagues can predispose you for such targeting by verbal abusers: your ear piercing, your tattoo, your religion (or lack thereof), your educational experience, your race, your gender, your accent, and so forth.

A first step in ending the verbal abuse that often flows toward "those with a difference" begins by getting the abuser to recognize and come to terms with the specifics of that difference. Here's a brief dialogue to make the point concretely:

EMPLOYEE: Mr. Wilson, you are on my case more often and more severely than any of the other first-year employees. I want to understand why.

SUPERVISOR: Oh, you do, do you? Well, for starters, you screw up more than anyone else.

EMPLOYEE: I sometimes make mistakes, but no more than most of my coworkers. Is there something about me that you don't like?

SUPERVISOR: I don't play favorites. I just call it like I see it. You could do yourself a lot of good by combing out those goofy cornrows on your head.

EMPLOYEE: This is about my hair?

SUPERVISOR: Of course not. I was just giving you some advice so you would fit in around here a lot better.

EMPLOYEE: Look, Mr. Wilson, I'm not wearing my hair in any particular style to bug you or anyone else. Here's the reason for cornrows and here are some of the mainstream people wearing them (goes on to educate boss about the hairstyle).

We're not pretending that these sorts of conversations instantly convert a bully into a pal. But at least the door is open for both sides to glimpse the real issues that are responsible for the conflict.

6. You may be perceived by a verbal abuser as socially or organizationally marginal. In this context, the traditional office delivery boy (typically a teenager who scurries from office to office with packages and messages) will probably get rougher verbal treatment during the day ("And be quick about it!") than will an employee farther up the ranks. Similarly, "temp" employees often complain that they are treated in a rude tone and peremptory manner not used on full-time employees.

Sociologists have studied the "lowest rung" factor in groups and societies. Each social group, no matter how poor or uneducated, wants to believe (and enforce the belief on others) that *someone* ranks below them in status and opportunity (and, they would go on to say, basic intelligence, morality, beauty, healthiness, and so forth.) German immigrants to the United States in the 1860s bemoaned their impoverished conditions, but consoled themselves that "at least we're not Irish." The Irish, of course, had their own chosen group to stand on top of.

Those who are perceived as the "lowest rung" members, whether among individuals or social groups, are more likely to draw abuse upon themselves, including verbal abuse. Abusers target these people because they are, by and large, less able to defend themselves and severely lacking in allies. No other social group stands willing to come to their rescue. (The long abuse of slaves in the United States, and the tragically slow evolution of the Anti-slave Movement, makes this point.)

If you regularly experience verbal abuse in a way that others in your workplace do not, you may want to examine your status in the pecking order of the company power structure. Are you in fact at, or near, the bottom—and are people treating you accordingly? Ironically, simply knowing that verbal abuse is coming your way primarily for "where I'm at on the ladder" can be a relief in some ways, especially if you imagined that the abuse was directed toward you for some personal attribute or failing. Recognizing why people feel free to verbally abuse you also puts you in a position to create strategies for ending such abuse. These are described in Chapter 10.

7. Verbal abuse may fall upon you in close coordination with certain environmental and circumstantial factors. "My boss never talks crudely to me at work," Rachel says, "but when we are out of the office on a sales call or

business trip he turns into a combination of a grouch and a letch. I think he wants attention from me in some form, and he doesn't mind at all if it is negative attention. So if we stop for coffee, he gripes to me that the coffee is too cold, and why did I choose this place. If we have a meal together, his is awful, and what am I trying to do, kill him with too much cholesterol? This goes on and on. He talks to me as if I were his slave wife ready to whimper over his every complaint or need. It's verbal abuse and I'm going to change jobs if it doesn't stop."

Behaviors such as those shown by this whining boss rarely stop on their own. Rachel may have to find the right moment to have a grown-up conversation with this overgrown infant. "Mr. Evans, you may be just joking about all the things you find unsatisfactory, too hot or too cold, too soft or too hard, or too early or too late on our business trips. But it's not funny to me and it makes me feel very used. I want to talk like adults on our trips and relate like employees in the same company. If we can't do that, I want to talk to HR and your boss about the problem and get their help in resolving it."

8. You may be the "wounded duck" or "bleeding fish" in your particular work pond. One of the sad realities of animal life is that the distressed creature, be it duck or tadpole, gets nipped, teased, and otherwise tormented by the stronger, healthier animals. Darwin no doubt had an explanation for this in terms of the strong breeders eliminating the weak breeders.

What works for ducks, fish, and Darwin is wholly inappropriate in the human sphere. If your work history has already branded you as the injured one (perhaps because of a demotion, a failed project, a notorious run-in with the boss, a forced transfer from another section, or whatever), you must be on guard against the "piling on" phenomenon—that is, the willingness of higher status employees to gang up on those who evidenced a weakness of some kind. The blood sport in your particular office may be to hound those who seem most needy and most afraid.

As a case in point, football stars cheered wildly by their fans meet a very different reception after they have fumbled the ball to lose a couple key games. The "injured" in any group have to create for themselves, or seek from others (perhaps HR), a protective shield that keeps them from being the butt of office jokes and the target of group abuse. Ways to find and use such a shield are explained in Chapter 10.

9. You may be selected for verbal abuse solely because you are the new kid on the block. In the animal world, horses (and virtually all other mammals) have developed elaborate "humble pie" behaviors they use when entering a herd or other animal group for the first time. The new horse will hang its head, tuck its tail between its legs, and avert its eyes and face from the other horses. This routine can go on for many days until, through a series of small steps, the dominant horses in the herd allow membership to the newcomer.

In your workgroup, your "newbie" status may attract a wide range of mildly abusive attacks, ranging from "You really don't know what you're doing, do you?" to "I'll tell you how to do it, but you won't remember, so ask me again tomorrow" to "Don't just sit there. At least pretend that you're doing something useful." Older, established workers say such obnoxious things to remind you of their superior status and to evoke "tail between legs" behavior from you. Frankly, they enjoy your discomfort as a newbie because it contrasts so pleasingly with their own feelings of mastery and security on the job.

The solution to the newbie dilemma usually does not lie in rebellion against the Old Guard and flaunting of all office conventions. Your ability to fend off abusive statements by humorous (but not glib) responses and your refusal to act helpless goes a long way toward ending this form of verbal abuse, as explained in more detail in Chapter 10.

Here's a brief dialogue to make the point:

OLD EMPLOYEE (half teasing): Well, what have we here? Wet behind the ears and waiting for lunch.

NEW EMPLOYEE (smiling): No, I'm not taking lunch. I have too much to do.

(Conversation then turns to what the new employee is working on. Talk moves away from abusive teasing and toward ordinary chat.)

10. Finally, you may be targeted for verbal abuse by those who believe you owe them something. In HBO's *The Sopranos*, the Mafia bosses always save their crudest insults and imprecations for those in debt to them. For example, Tony Soprano would find it easy to say, "Christopher, you son of a bitch, I went out on a limb for you and this is how you repay me."

Similarly, in business practice, your mentors and guardian angels in the company can easily become your verbal tormentors. Like James Bond, they feel they have not so much a "right to kill" as a "right to verbally abuse."

A male mentor who brought a woman into the business on his personal recommendation may make the mistake of relaxing ordinary business limits in conversation: "So, sweetheart, how are things going so far? Do you want to have lunch just to talk?"

A female mentor might make a different mistake with the same young woman: "I told you to watch yourself with him. He's not to be trusted. Check with me about these things. In fact, don't make any moves without talking to me. I'll steer you right. If you mess up, it's on both of us." This kind of talk, while marginally abusive to the dignity and independence of the young woman, can become overtly abusive if she does in fact make a wrong move. Then the hammer comes down: "Damn it, I told you always to check with me!"

Verbal Abuse and Gender

Based on complaints of verbal abuse across industries, we can conclude that women are targets of verbal abuse about twice as often as men are. By exploring reasons for these differences, we can equip ourselves with insights for stopping verbal abuse in its tracks, whether aimed at women or men.

As Dr. Pat Heim and other gender experts have written, women in organizations value relationships more than power levels. They go out of their way to nurture good feelings, and to make each woman in the group feel valued. (This generalization does not, of course, describe all workplaces.) If a woman manager is giving an assignment to a female subordinate, she is likely to ask the subordinate her thoughts on how the assignment can best be accomplished. Expectations are negotiated so that neither woman feels "one down."[1]

Harsh, commanding language that breaks into this relationship environment is seen by women as abusive because it violates the fabric of relationship they have worked hard to establish and maintain. Abusive language inevitably communicates that one or more people in the group is devalued—an unacceptable thought for a nurturing circle of women. When verbal abuse occurs, women will typically come to the abused person's aid more quickly than will men. This aid takes the form of expressions of empathy, offers to "be there" if the person needs to talk, and suggestions of counteractions that the person can take against the verbal abuser.

In addition, men and women handle and express their response to angry attacks (as in the case of verbal abuse) in quite different ways. Women who are verbally attacked will often express their reaction in an inward-directed way ("Let me tell you how I felt when he said that"). Here the focus is on the woman's feelings, not the abuser's actions. A man in a similar circumstance will be more likely to express his response in an outward-directed way ("Here's what that SOB said/did to me"). In this case, the focus is on the perpetrator's actions, rather than the victim's feelings.

Finally, women and men in the same group will behave differently. Women are more than twice as likely to laugh, smile, and show other signs of happiness in a male/female group. Men are more likely to engage in mock attack teasing, first directed at one another, and gradually at women who are accepted as part of the group.

For example, take a group of men standing in the hall of an office. Their banter focuses on putdowns of one another, with the goal of humorous effect and bonding. One man says to the other, "Are they still letting you on the golf course?" The other man responds, "They found out I played a round with you, so I'm banished for life." Both men chuckle. The joke wasn't particularly funny, but it gives them a chance to spar in a teasing way and thereby show interest and fondness for one another.

Now consider what happens when a woman, Olivia, approaches the group. She smiles and engages the male members of the group by questions, not statements: "So how is it going?" No matter what the men say in response, she laughs lightly, as if delighted by their answers. In the course of 15 minutes or more with the group, she will tend to smile much more often than any man in the group and play the role of interested audience member, rather than conversation initiator. Her questions may occasionally start conversation topics, but it will be up to the men to provide the answers and content for the topic at hand. She contributes phrases such as, "That's really interesting!" and "I didn't know that."

Women who are thoroughly accepted into this male/female circle will be included in mock teasing—and it is here that some verbal abuse takes place. One male member, thinking he is being clever, may say to a female member of the group, "I see you are wearing your FM (high heel) shoes today." When asked what "FM" means, he whispers loudly, "Fuck Me Shoes" and laughs. The woman may laugh at the moment, but she also realizes that the door is now open for explicit sexual banter, at least with this man, whenever she wears a particular pair of high heels to work. In fact, she doesn't know quite what to do with his off-color joke. On the one hand, she is complimented by being included in the boys' club, and recognizes that teasing humor is a sign of their acceptance of her as an equal. On the other hand, she knows that their mock attack humor will always be aimed at a putdown, which is anathema to women seeking environments of nurturing relationships rather power hierarchies.

This essential conflict between what men want from one another (bonds based on acknowledgment of a pecking order, arranged by status and abilities) and what women want from one another (nurturing relationships that keep all members of the group contented and safe) gives rise to many instances of verbal abuse. "Men's talk" is understood (men would say misunderstood) in some women's groups as offensive, insulting, and denigrating. This is the same language men appreciated as virile, challenging, and invigorating. At Sun Microsystems, CEO Scott McNealy at one point announced that the informal motto of the company would be, "Kick Butt and Have Fun." It's not known if women in the organization found quite the humor and energy in that motto that McNealy and his male associates intended.

This information about gender differences in the perception of language should alert men to exercise caution in messages they send to groups that include women (and, for that matter, men who aren't into the macho aspects of their gender). Particular care should be used when speaking to women who have been brought into the inner circle of our male-dominated business society. These women are too often treated as "one of the guys," which includes being subjected to language attacks that would peel wallpaper. Women often react to such language environments by backing away from membership in the boys' club, or by faking an appreciative response that quickly proves insincere. (Admittedly, some women thrive in the environment described here, and no judgment is intended about their femininity or continuing relations with other women in the organization.)

Similarly, women who interface with an occasional man in their workplace can expect him to be less quick to say and do nurturing things to build relationships. He may be more likely to give commands rather than to ask about opinions and feelings. He may use signs of temper and expressions of ultimatums ("It has to be done by Friday" rather than "How does Friday look to you? Can you squeeze this in? I would really appreciate it."). Rather than feeling abused by his male-centered approach to communication, women can learn to recognize his tendencies and translate them, when possible, into messages that are more acceptable to the group of women involved. Some male bosses, in fact, end up using a female executive assistant as a liaison to communicate with a largely female workforce.

Chapter 3

Why Them? Profiles of Verbal Abusers

Throughout this book, verbal abusers have most often been cast as people in positions of organizational power. Directors, bosses, managers, supervisors, division or department heads, and team leaders all stand, figuratively, like Zeus at the edge of heaven ready to throw down lightning bolts in the form of verbal abuse. As we will see, the direction for verbal abuse does not always follow the pecking order within a company. But those in power often become guilty of verbal abuse because they spend so much time in downward communication—telling people (through e-mails, phone calls, in person conferences, and during all kinds of meetings) *what to do*. When these directions come in the context of a company crisis or urgent market opportunity, a considerable degree of emotion can accompany them. And when that emotion boils over into impatience and anger, verbal abuse quickly ensues.

Some enlightened bosses do not perceive their primary duty as giving orders. Instead, they take a portion of their day to *listen* to what others think and feel. These moments of information gathering, rather than information dissemination, can prove to be a powerful antidote against the temptation to verbally abuse others. A Greek philosopher proposed that, "God gave us two ears and one mouth. They should be used in that proportion."

Verbal Abuse for Theory X and Theory Y Managers

In *The Human Side of Enterprise*, management guru Douglas Macgregor proposed two polar opposites in management style, which he termed Theory X management and Theory Y management. For reasons that will become clear, Theory X managers are much more likely to indulge in verbal abuse than are Theory Y managers. After all, according to Macgregor, Theory X managers make the following assumptions about the people they supervise:

- Workers are innately lazy and need to be driven by the stick of fear.

- Workers are out only for what they can get from the company, not what they can give to the company.

- Work itself is essentially stultifying and painful, and is undertaken only because of economic necessity.

- An inevitable antagonism exists between the leader and those led, just as circus lions growl at the man with the whip.[1]

Coming from this set of assumptions, it is little wonder that Theory X managers often find themselves in verbal conflict with their employees. As one manager put it, "I'm the only one in my office who wants to see work get done well and on time. If it weren't for the pressure I put on my people every hour of every day, things would quickly go to hell in a hand basket." In rebuttal, one of this manager's employees tells the other side of the story: "He thinks he has all the good ideas and the rest of us are dolts. He makes unreasonable demands based on schedules and deadlines he has invented. No wonder we all hate the guy. He hates us!"

Theory X management is alive and well, both inside the United States and internationally. Another name for this management style is "MGM"—Management by Getting Mad. The boss perceives his responsibility as pushing the performance of his people with the ramrod of his anger and impatience. "I yell and they jump," one MGM manager says. "If I don't yell, they just sit there."

Many management studies have demonstrated that a boss's display of anger can produce short-term motivation for workers. For example, a boss's tirade can make employees take only their allowed coffee breaks, and not a minute more. But that same tirade cannot motivate employees to offer more creative ideas, work together more cohesively, or develop feelings of loyalty and commitment to the company.

Macgregor therefore argued for the value of an alternative management style, the Theory Y approach. Managers taking this approach make quite different assumptions about work and those they supervise. Rather than more negative, Theory X assumptions, Theory Y managers assume the following:

- Work can be interesting, enjoyable, fulfilling, and almost indistinguishable at times from hobbies and play.

- Workers are intelligent and like to participate in problem solving.

- Workers can form congenial relations with company leaders, since both parties are in partnership to achieve mutual goals for themselves and the company.

- Workers bring considerable energy and good intentions to their jobs, and need to be rewarded far more often than disciplined.

Managers operating from the Theory Y perspective seldom find themselves in verbal spats with their subordinates. When disagreements occur, those differences are a stimulus to discussion and negotiation, not angry commands and demeaning criticism. Although Theory Y managers may feel the same amount of passion for their jobs as Theory X managers, they express that passion in the form of enthusiasm, support, and optimism rather than discouragement, character assassination, and pessimism.

Verbal Abusers Explain Themselves

In the course of researching this book, I had the opportunity to speak at length with more than 60 recovering verbal abusers, most of them managers and supervisors, from a dozen or so different companies. Two thirds of these individuals were male. All were involved in company programs or company outsourced counseling programs to help them understand why they had resorted to verbal abuse in the workplace and to build new, more constructive skill sets for working with others.

As these men and women, both individually and in small focus groups, reflected on the reasons and impulses that led them to verbally abusive behavior, they revealed factors that we all should take to heart (as company leaders, regular employees, and victims of verbal abuse), in our efforts to stop verbal abuse at its many sources.

Here, in the combined words of these individuals, are seven explanations (but not justifications) for their previous verbal abuse of others in the workplace:

1. *"It's how I kept control of my employees.* I didn't really know any other way, since I had come up through the ranks, with tough bosses over me all the way. I basically thought that a boss was supposed to be mean so that his employees didn't try to get away with stuff on the job. Looking back, that's pretty much how my father was to my brothers and me—hard, unsympathetic, unbending. When I got my first management job, I told my employees that I was

not running a popularity contest and I didn't particularly care whether they liked me or not. My responsibility was to get the job done."

2. *"I had old debts to pay.* I was passed over for promotion three times because of a few backstabbing people with whom I worked. I promised myself that if I ever got to be manager, they would pay. And I've kept my promise."

3. *"I thought the stick would work better than the carrot.* When I got really tough in the way I talked to some of my employees, I thought at the time that I was doing the company a favor. I figured that they would take their jobs more seriously and work harder if I showed that I wouldn't take any crap and had no interest in their sob stories. Besides, the company was going through hard financial times, and as managers we didn't have many carrots to offer to employees. When you don't have carrots, you only have the stick as a motivator. At least that's what I thought at the time."

4. *"I didn't know how to deal with my own anger.* Anger management classes have become something of a joke on TV now, but I really needed one. When something went wrong for me as a supervisor, my first impulse was to kick those beneath me. I guess misery loves company. I remember one time when I received a mediocre performance evaluation and didn't get the raise my wife and I were counting on. I stormed around the office for a week and bawled out at least four of my subordinates for what now seems like small potatoes."

5. *"I was bored and a bit sadistic.* This isn't a good thing to admit, but I got some pleasure out of watching people squirm, especially if I thought they deserved it for some reason. I guess my pet peeve was new employees who had never done an honest day's work in their lives—you know, the kids just out of fancy schools. I made it my personal mission to acquaint them with the School of Hard Knocks, where I was 'educated.' I didn't let their mistakes pass easily, but pretty much reamed them out whenever they slipped up."

6. *"I was acting a part for the people upstairs who were watching me.* My bosses gave me this department and told me to straighten it out. I managed my people the same way I was being managed. When my bosses didn't like what I was doing, I was called to the carpet in the executive wing for a tongue-lashing. That's the same management technique I used when my people screwed up. It wasn't really me, as I told my wife many times. It was just a role that I played because that's what I thought my bosses expected."

7. *"Some people just rubbed me the wrong way.* I have a kind of chemistry thing that goes on between me and people that I meet, including people that work for me. Some people I like immediately and they like me. But others strike me as stuck up, antisocial, or prudes. In those cases, I have trouble holding myself back from letting them know what I think about them. I mean, most of them have gone through their whole lives without someone looking them in the eye and asking them whether they really believe their own bull. I had the same reaction to people in high school.

You can find phony people everywhere and they are really hard to take, at least for me."

The individuals behind these words are committed to changing their perspectives and interpersonal communication approaches as managers. Their words, however, give us insights into what makes a verbal abuser "tick." Too often we allow the title of a verbal abuser—"vice president," "division head," "chief officer," "department manager," and so forth—to convince ourselves that he or she must be seeing the world correctly, and that we are the guilty ones with the skewed vision of things. These brief testimonials make just the opposite case: the verbal abuser comes to the incident with a warped view of what it means to manage others, or simply to work side by side with them. The abuser has the problem, no matter how hard he or she tries to convince us that the problem is ours alone.

Men and Verbal Abuse

American business, particularly at the upper echelons of CEOs, vice presidents, senior executives, and members of the board, is still male-dominated. For all the visibility of outstanding female leaders in some well-known firms, women make up less than 1 percent of CEOs in Fortune 500 companies, less than 16 percent of partner-level lawyers, and less than 7 percent of top-earning doctors.[2]

As the Infoplease Daily Almanac for April 21, 2005 points out, "although women make up almost half of America's labor force, still only two Fortune 500 companies have women CEOs or presidents, and 90 of those 500 companies don't have *any* women corporate officers.[3]

In this male environment, patterns of speech emerge between men that too often become the common communication mode of the company itself. Men typically (though often unconsciously) strive for dominance, or "one-up" status, in relationships. In conversation with one another, they often attempt to "out tough" one another by statements of violent action ("We'll kick their butts!"), strong expressions of macho emotion ("What in the hell do they think they're doing!"), and pithy labels for others ("Bastards!").

Such bluster can be interpreted as warrior talk, the stomping and shouting around the fire to rouse one's courage in preparation for battle. Or the same blather can be understood as one-upmanship, with bulls banging their words together instead of their horns in a ritual battle for male status and supremacy. Even our business magazines play into this use of business language, with regular articles on "The Ten Toughest Bosses in America" and "The Most Unpopular, Most Successful Business Leaders."

Men in business have so thoroughly embraced "tough talk" as their mode of communication that they even use it to express affection. One manager picking up a male friend at the airport shouts out, "You sorry son of a bitch. You look like hell," as a way of expressing a more mundane sentiment ("Hi. How was your trip?") At retirement ceremonies (usually turned into "roasts," if men have anything to say about the proceedings), beloved figures are reminded of their mistakes, mock attacked for their pretensions, and called by more than one four-letter word during the course of the evening.

Men who swim in the sea of such mano y mano language become inured to it. They do not realize its impact on others outside the "code circle." Viewed schematically, they have encoded certain words ("asshole," "jerk off") with special meanings they anticipate will be decoded correctly, as intended, by the message receiver. For example, one male worker, Tom, sends an e-mail to another male friend in the company. "I need those specs—unless you want to be an asshole about it and make me look like a jerk off to my boss. See you at lunch." The male friend decodes these words with a smile, not a frown. The use of strong language is interpreted as mock-teasing.

The Mathematical Theory of Communication

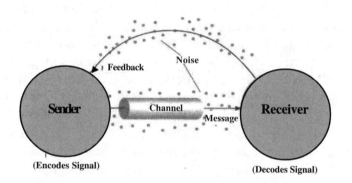

But what about those who aren't in on the joke—those who aren't decoding messages encoded by male rules? Consider Linda, for example. She also receives a message from Tom: "Linda, I'm getting those specs this afternoon and I need you to get your ass in gear to review them before quitting time today, okay?" Linda is confused. Is Tom angry at her? Is he joking? Is he disparaging her working habits? Worse, is he coming on to her in some odd way?

Of course, most men manage to turn off their male buddy code language for audiences of nonmembers (including women, men with whom they are not friends, and most bosses above them in the power hierarchy). These people will tend to receive vanilla messages without raw language. But, interestingly, once a nonmember has been brought into the "club," so to speak, by frequent, friendly contact and, perhaps, business lunches or drinks after work, that nonmember starts to receive the full flow of "in group" language: off-color jokes, mock attacks using otherwise taboo words ("Linda, you beeatchy woman!"), and strong, coarse language in ordinary messaging. These uses of language are, in fact, a sign of trust from the group—"we know that you understand our humor and are part of the cool group"— and also a reminder of her status as an insider—"we only talk this way to people we like."

But here's the point with regard to verbal abuse: Linda, or any former nonmember of an "in" group at work, may not have chosen to become a "language intimate" (in terms of the unrestricted use of foul language) simply by becoming friendly with others at work. In fact, she may not have initiated those friendly relationships. Men in organizations often select nonmembers such as Linda to befriend in a one-way act of relationship creation. (Linda starts being treated as an "in" group member even if she has not chosen such membership on her own.)

Especially in these cases, where the crude use of language by the "in" group isn't fully understood or adequately interpreted by the new member, the experience of verbal abuse can occur, and often in severe ways. Linda may wonder why other employees, most of them men, are taking her aside to tell her the latest off-color joke. She may not appreciate passing comments about her clothing, figure, makeup ("Linda, those bedroom eyes!"), and other personal attributes.

In short, Linda finds herself not so much angry as confused. "I used to come to work kind of in a neutral mood— it was just work, and I did it as well as I could and then came home to my real life. But now when I go to work I dread the jokes, the comments, and the foul language. I know these people don't mean anything by it—it's just the way they talk to each other at work. But I didn't ask for this and it makes me feel uncomfortable. I just want to go back to the way my job used to be, with people talking to one another in ordinary, friendly ways without a lot of inappropriate stuff. It makes me feel cheap to be talked to in this way."

Chapter 4

Verbal Abuse, the Courts, and Company Codes

Abuse can take many forms in the workplace, and it's useful to understand verbal abuse as part of that larger picture. Consider these six forms of workplace abuse, not all of which are adequately covered by company guidelines or regulations:

1. *Organizational abuse.* Your company may err—and, in so doing, abuse your interests—by assigning you to the wrong job in the wrong place at the wrong time. Through organizational mistakes, for example, an excellent software engineer can find herself hating her assigned "promotion" as a department manager.

2. *Abuse through neglect.* Your company may have tabbed "fast trackers" within your work group and left the remaining employees to wither on the vine, without equal access to training, high visibility projects, and company social occasions ("cocktails with the company president," and so forth).

3. *Social abuse.* In all human groups over time, cliques emerge and people play favorites. Through no fault of your own, you can find yourself in the "out" group, with negative implications for your career path.

4. *Emotional or psychological abuse.* Closely akin to verbal abuse (because incidents of emotional and psychological abuse inevitably involve communication), these forms of abuse tear down the individuality and "personhood" of the victim. His or her anxieties are awakened by threats of hostility, job loss, or relocation; the heat of those anxieties is then fanned to an all consuming point by frequent nagging, teasing, harsh words, and humiliating treatment. Workers who have somehow become the targets of a vengeful boss's anger often become victims of emotional or psychological abuse: "I can't fire her, but I can make her life hell as long as she works for me."

5. *Physical abuse.* Although we are almost a century beyond the last common workplace occurrences of beating, strapping, and confinement as penalties for mistakes at work, some aspects of physical abuse are still tolerated and even encouraged in some organizations. Intern physicians, for example, are routinely given 24 to 30 hour shifts, with resulting physical fatigue so severe that some states are investigating whether these men and women are fit to drive home. Truck drivers, similarly, are often pressured by shippers to break union and safety guidelines for marathon driving stints that endanger their own health and that of others on the road.

6. *Verbal abuse.* This form of abuse has been called "a whipping with words." The primary purpose of verbal abuse, from the viewpoint of the abuser, is to inflict pain, not to bring about constructive change or to better working relationships. Verbal abuse typically demeans the targeted person in the process of criticizing his or her performance. The victim feels personally attacked, rather than professionally assessed.

Laws for Verbal Abuse vs. Laws for Sexual Harassment

It's instructive to compare the elaborate federal and state laws, industry guidelines, and company regulations surrounding sexual harassment (which often combines verbal and physical abuse) with the relatively small body of legislation and rule pertaining to verbal abuse.

With Fortune 500 companies expending an average of $6.7 million in legal judgments and expenses stemming from harassment[1], virtually every large corporation has spelled out exactly for its workers what constitutes sexual harassment, what a victim should do, and what will happen to the perpetrator. In most cases, a single harassing act (a hand placed inappropriately on a knee, for example) can set in motion a virtual machine of fact gathering, employee interviews, disciplinary procedures, and reparations. Even the use of the word "sexual harassment" has a chilling effect on would-be office Romeos, stopping them in their tracks if they value their careers.

Not so with verbal abuse. The concept is relatively new to American business and definitely has not trickled down to most line managers. A verbal abuser whose victim retorts, "You're verbally abusing me!" may not miss a beat in continuing his verbal assault. Beyond general statements regarding "respect for the dignity of each individual," most corporate employee handbooks do not contain specific policies or warnings about verbal abuse in the workplace.

Consider the following example: Your boss's rant, filled with foul language, has been going on for ten minutes. You put your foot down and say, "If you continue to speak to me that way, I'll...I'll sue you!"

Well, yes and no. Although the story is a bit long to tell, regulations pertaining to verbal abuse are much more defined at the company level than in federal and state courts. As Employment Attorney Tim Willoughby puts it, "There is no law that mandates that the employer be courteous and decent. But there are laws that forbid certain kinds of mistreatment under certain circumstances."[2]

Let's take a real world example of Willoughby's point. A woman contacts an attorney online with this situation: "I work in a salaried position where I have been for five years. In the last two to three years, my supervisor has gotten worse and worse, messing things up and then threatening to fire everyone for not getting him out of a jam. He constantly talks in foul language, swearing all of the time. He is notorious for making racial slurs.... He is now preparing for employee evaluations and the threats just keep on coming.... What constitutes the development of a 'hostile work environment' outside of the sexual harassment laws? Is there an actionable event here?"

The attorney responds, "No, there is nothing actionable here. This is not a hostile work environment in the legal meaning of the phrase. Your boss has apparently turned into an abusive lunatic, but that is not against the law. No laws require the boss to be nice, or even sane. If you think it will do any good, you are free to speak to someone in more senior management about the situation and see if they will address the problem. Failing that, your option is to seek new employment elsewhere."[3]

Ouch! We would have guessed that the boss's language and manner qualified as classic verbal abuse. Aren't there strict laws against verbal abuse in the workplace?

The Evolution of Verbal Abuse Law

The great majority of laws pertaining to harassment and abuse arise out of Title VII of the Civil Rights Act of 1964. There, the focus is primarily on discrimination. In fact, most anti-discrimination legislation does not make use of the words "harassment" or "abuse." Twenty years after Title VII appeared, only 3 percent of all claims within the discrimination category had to do with harassment, and virtually none of those with nonsexual verbal abuse.[4]

Later court rulings, especially Harris v. Forklist Systems, Inc. (1993), and activism by the EEOC gave specific guidelines for what did or did not constitute harassment. (Harassment claims quickly rose thereafter to their present level of about 18 percent of all discrimination filings.)[5]

These rulings combined to describe harassment punishable by law as "severe or pervasive" in the workplace, with the result that a "hostile or abusive work environment" is created. Harassment must be based on race, religion, sex, national origin, age, disability, or veteran status. In some regions, sexual orientation, citizenship, marital status, political affiliation, and personal appearance are also included. Finally, the harassment must be apparent in a subjective way to the plaintiff (or victim) and in an objective way to what the courts called "a reasonable person."

The courts have never ruled that obscenity, profanity, or downright rudeness in the private workplace are actionable as primary evidence of a hostile work environment. "The workplace is not a place by law mandated to be free of vulgarity," writes Richard K. Berger, president and senior counsel of Berkent Legal Services in Massachusetts. With regard to federal laws, Berger points out that unless the language is sexually charged, harassment laws don't provide for work environments devoid of foul language.[6]

Walking through any factory, warehouse, or assembly plant in 2005 would make Berger's point in a vivid way. A recent University of North Carolina Business School survey, "Workplace Incivility: the Target's Eye View," reveals that 78 percent of those surveyed believed that rudeness and incivility in the workplace are worse now than 10 years ago. The study found that 12 percent of those who had experienced significant incivility and rudeness quit their jobs. A not surprising 52 percent admitted that they had lost work time in various ways due to worrying about being a victim or target of another person's rudeness.[7]

Five studies reported in *The Wall Street Journal* also examined the pervasiveness of obscenity in American workplaces. In one survey of 12,000 U.S. Postal Service employees, for example, 43 percent reported being cursed at in the workplace.[8]

Employment attorney Jonathan Segal points out that, for employees of private companies, "there are generally not the same First Amendment issues" to freedom of speech, including profanity. For that reason, companies like Texas-based Ramtech Building Systems enforces a strict policy against "unwanted, deliberate, repeated, unsolicited profanity, cussing, swearing, vulgar, insulting, abusive or crude language."[9] Those who violate the policy face disciplinary procedures, including required counseling or termination.

In summary, your most available and potentially successful route of complaint as a victim of verbal abuse may not be to the courts (unless the abuse altered the conditions of your employment in a "severe or pervasive" way so as to produce a "hostile work environment," *and* was based upon race, religion, sex, national origin, age, disability, veteran status, or, in some jurisdictions, sexual orientation, citizenship, marital status, political affiliation, and personal appearance). In a long series of rulings, both federal and state courts have demonstrated that they do not consider one or two run-ins with, let's say, a belligerent boss or a coworker who calls you a gender-based vulgar name, to be sufficient grounds for a finding of harassment and abuse. (However, if those isolated acts were combined with physical violence in any form, the courts have been much more likely to rule for the plaintiff.)

When Title VII protected areas are violated, especially by an employer or through an employer's benign neglect, courts and government agencies have come down hard. Eugene Volokh, Acting Professor at the University of California, Los Angles School of Law, summarizes several such cases:

- "A state court has in fact found that it was religious harassment for an employer to put religious articles in its employee newsletter and Christian-themed verses on its paychecks. The EEOC likewise found that a claim that an employer 'permitted the daily broadcast of prayers over its public address system' over the span of a year was 'sufficient to allege the existence of a hostile working environment predicated on religious discrimination.'"

- "A state administrative agency has found that an employee was religiously harassed by a Seventh Day Adventist coworker who often talked about religion to everyone."

- "One court has said that coworkers' use of job titles such as 'foreman' and 'draftsman' may constitute sexual harassment, and a Kentucky human rights agency has gotten a company to change its 'Men Working' signs (at a cost of more than $35,000) on the theory that the signs 'perpetuate a discriminatory work environment.'"

- "The Office of Federal Compliance Programs characterized anti-veteran postings at Ohio State University as harassment based on Vietnam-era veteran status ... [I]n one of the departments professors displayed inflammatory pictures and postings, offensive to Vietnam-era veterans on their office windows facing the corridors."[10]

In an additional case not reviewed by Professor Volokh, the Minnesota Library had to pay $435,000 to 12 of its librarians who complained that library users brought up sexually explicit images on the Internet screens of library computers, images to which the library staff was inevitably exposed. The court ruled that they were enduring a hostile work environment and ordered the University to place strict controls on the computers available to library patrons.[11]

The upshot of these kinds of cases for employers is to be hyper-vigilant about any communications, written or spoken, that might be construed as harassing or abusive. As concluded by the *Employee Relations Law Journal,* "An employer's incentive to prohibit conduct and speech that might constitute harassment has increased based on the Civil Rights Act of 1991, which subjects employers to liability for emotional distress and punitive damages. To avoid liability, the prudent employer will proscribe all speech and conduct that may constitute harassment. The possibility of creating a 'chilling effect' from prohibiting speech and conduct that may constitute harassment is outweighed by the risk of significant liability."[12]

Employers to the Rescue With Codes of Conduct

In an unusual reversal of traditional government/business relations, private employers have gone far beyond the guidelines of the court in setting forth work rules for their employees. These regulations are not "nice to have" behaviors that are optional for the workers, but instead are stringently enforced rules, with termination of the offender as a frequent option.

To gauge the wide coverage of potentially abusive language and acts covered by such policies, consider the code of conduct given to all employees of BlueCross BlueShield of Illinois:

"We are committed to maintaining a work environment where we treat each other with honesty, dignity, and respect. We value the diverse contributions of all people, regardless of their position, sexual preference, family status, age, race, sex, disability, religion or national origin. All employment practices are based on ability and performance.... The Company will not tolerate sexual advances, actions, comments, inappropriate physical contact or any other conduct that is intimidating or otherwise creates an offensive or hostile work environment."[13]

At the University of California, Davis, a similar code gives "examples of behaviors that create a hostile work environment:

◆   Offcolor jokes or teasing.

◆   Comments about body parts or sex life.

◆   Suggestive pictures, poster, calendars or cartoons.

◆   Leering, stares or gestures.

◆   Touching—brushes, pats, hugs, shoulder rubs, or pinches."

The same code lists sample names and phrases that "create an intimidating, hostile or offensive work environment:

◆   Prude

◆   Frigid

◆   Gay

◆   Tease

◆   You just want attention, and you know you like it."[14]

The State of New Jersey includes these paragraphs in its Policy Prohibiting Discrimination:

"Unlawful discrimination/harassment undermines the integrity of the employment relationship, compromises equal employment opportunity, debilitates morale and interferes with work productivity. This policy applies to all employees and applicants for employment in State departments, commissions, colleges, and authorities. The State of New Jersey will not tolerate harassment or discrimination by anyone in the workplace including supervisors, coworkers, or nonemployees. This policy applies to conduct which occurs in the workplace, and also extends to conduct which occurs at any location that can be reasonably regarded as an extension of the workplace, such as any field location, any offsite business related social function, or any facility where State business is being conducted and discussed."

This policy also applies to third party harassment. Third party harassment is unwelcome behavior of a sexual, racial or derogatory nature regarding any protected category, that is not directed at an individual but is a part of that individual's work environment. Third party harassment based upon any of the aforementioned protected categories is prohibited by this policy.[15]

These examples suggest some of the ways in which employers of all types have extended existent guidelines to prevent even the hint of employer complicity or negligence in areas of sexual and verbal harassment and abuse. In effect, these employers have redefined "hostile workplace environment" to more closely resemble the description offered by the online journal, *Hostile Workplace Prevention*:

"A 'hostile workplace' is one where people can not do their best work or be their most productive due to conditions in their workplace. That is, the workplace is hostile to their natural humanity. Notice also the results of a hostile workplace are hostility toward the company's productivity, which directly impacts profits in a negative way. People who are unhappy, unhealthy, or angry do not work hard. A hostile workplace is the result of suppression of people's natural ability to express themselves. It is the opposite of a workplace that promotes creativity and vitality. Hostile workplaces are deadly to productivity. They are unhealthy—and potentially deadly—to the people who work there.

Hostility consists of:

♦   Verbal abuse against any person, for whatever reason.

♦   Angry interchanges between people over political or territorial boundaries.

♦   One-upmanship and excessive competition.

♦   Power plays and challenges issued over imagined threats to a person's authority.

♦   Attempts to squash a person's ability to be creative and to their best work in a way that is most productive for the individual.

♦   Enforcement of ineffective or unreasonable rules for the sole purpose of exerting power over others or to impede progress."[16]

Clearly, many of these guidelines will not now be enforced by law. It is reassuring that victims of verbal abuse and other forms of harassment often have a better chance for prompt, fair, and inexpensive action on their claims by contacting senior authorities within their companies than by pinning their hopes for justice on a protracted law suit.

Policies and Training Programs on Verbal Abuse

Notwithstanding the excellent policies we have discussed so far, relatively few companies have developed thorough policies which define verbal abuse, instruct employees on how to avoid it, and provide channels and mechanisms to act quickly and fairly when it does occur. Even fewer companies have designed training sessions for managers and other employees on the dangers of verbal abuse and strategies for eliminating it from the workplace.

We can address that vacuum in a tentative way by suggesting the following policy statement, at least in its core elements, for inclusion in company employee handbooks—and, better, in the forefront of executive minds and priorities for the company:

"This company values and expects courteous, civil communication among employees at all levels, no matter how urgent the problem at hand or how different the priorities, attitudes, and levels of authority of those communicating. We work best together when our language demonstrates our respect for one another's dignity and diversity as individuals and professionalism as employees. Language that violates these principles in tone or content is expressly banned by the company."

A one-day workshop for managers and other employees on verbal abuse might follow this approximate curriculum:

Introduction: What verbal abuse is, and why it matters to the company and its employees.

Roleplay: Three versions of manager/subordinate verbal abuse, followed by discussion of:

◆   The signs of verbal abuse.

◆   The victim's immediate response to verbal abuse.

Roleplay: Three versions of worker/coworker verbal abuse, followed by discussion of:

◆   Common situations where verbal abuse is likely to occur.

◆   The aftermath of verbal abuse for the participants and observers in the work group.

Review of Policies and Procedures Pertaining to Verbal Abuse:

◆   The company's position.

◆   Channels for filing complaints.

◆   Procedures for investigating and adjudicating incidents of verbal abuse.

Ten Tips on Avoiding Verbal Abuse as a Manager

Coaching Suggestions for Working with Employees Prone to Verbal Abuse

Counseling Suggestions for Helping Victims of Verbal Abuse in the Workforce

Setting the Record Straight About Profanity and Foul Language

If any of us were to move backward in time 200 or 300 years, we would find ourselves (no matter where we were in the world) in theocentric societies—that is, societies where God was almost constantly on the minds of people. Concern for God's will and fear of God's punishment dictated what one read, what one did (particularly on worship days), how one dressed, and how one brought infants into the world (with baptism, in some religions) and sent the elderly out of the world (with prayers, rituals, and blessings).

In earlier eras, the name of the god was considered magical and could only be used by priests when performing rites and incantations. To speak of the god figure in a casual, glib, or disrespectful way risked the imminent danger (the priests would say the certainty) of being struck by lightning, attacked by wild animals, or worse. An entire community could attribute the failure of crops or the absence of rain to the mistake of one member in uttering the name of the god amiss. Many of our odd distortions of religious names and terms (Jeez for Jesus, darn for damn, heck for hell, Jiminy Cricket for Jesus Christ, Holy Cow for Holy Ghost, and goldarnit for God damn it, to name a few) hearken back to the same motive of avoiding bad fortune by not speaking the name of the god.

In that kind of world, you can imagine the expressive power of "using God's name in vain"—that is, attaching God's name to such expressions as "God damn" and "For Christ's sake" and even "in Heaven's name." One's use of such culturally risky phrases indicated to all listeners the intensity of one's feelings—in effect, the lengths to which one was willing to go (even risking damnation) to press a particular point. For example, if a farmer told his farm-hand to, "go fetch that godforsaken bull," the farmer was breaking the taboo of not using God's name in vain, but with the purpose of creating an especially strong impression for the farmhand. As a general rule, it can be said that, in those days, attaching the name of the deity to any common expression marked the speaker as somewhat of a moral rebel, capable of strong actions to match his strong words.

Swear words and curse words had a similar potency for branding messages as urgent and usually angry. "I swear to God, John, you'd better help me get this crop to market" was a strong expression of exasperation. The most drastic of the curses (such as "The devil take you" and "You can go to hell") were dramatic ways of cutting off all relationship with a person, or at least threatening to do so. The word "damn" became a shorthand way of invoking the taboo use of full curses—"God damn you to hell" would be the completely stated curse. So when a patron tells a bartender in a Western movie to "give me another damn whisky," he is branding himself as a moral outsider and angry or depressed soul who doesn't hesitate to shake his fist at God in the course of ordering a drink. Swearing and cursing became synonymous with bravado.

When breaking the taboo against using God's name did not create sufficient impressions of anger and dark intentions in a message, an additional cultural taboo could be pressed into service. Most cultures that have developed "polite" societies have also circumscribed some barnyard or bedroom words as beyond the pale of civilized discourse. Bringing these taboo words—that is, foul language—into one's speaking indicated that you were willing to stand apart from the society's pretensions and "cut through the bull." The long list of slang words for excrement, intercourse, bowel and bladder habits, sexual body parts, and so forth became commonplace at first among the disenfranchised masses who could care less about polite society, and later by members of the upper crust who wanted to capture the energy, sense of abandon, and purposeful notoriety.

To counter the risk that God's name would inadvertently be used inappropriately, some religions (notably Judaism) required that the name of God not be written out completely, but instead captured as a series of letters with an asterisk or hyphen in place of one or more missing letters. So "God" in many Jewish prayer books and other worship or study materials is transcribed as Gd or G*d.

Modern publishers, particularly for school audiences, have done something similar with foul language, inserting a place holding character in words such as f*ck and sh*t so as not to be accused of publishing banned words.

That quick sketch of how swear words came to find an important place in our speaking and writing brings us to their use in modern business cultures. As a very general rule, swearing at an employee or using swear words (particularly highly taboo words such as "fuck") provides a positive litmus test for verbal abuse. A manager simply can't tell a secretary to "get your goddamn feet off the desk and do some frigging work for a change!" without risking an immediate diminution in his reputation as a manager and possible follow-up discipline from the company (or in extreme cases, from the courts).

The exceptions to this general rule are many. Senior executives behind closed doors are legendary for their fulsome use of foul language, as if they had been saving it up until they were alone together in a secure chamber. Managers at all levels have been known to drop in an occasional "damn" or "hell" for peppery effect in speeches and briefings without the moral universe collapsing. Also common (perhaps too common) is resorting to name-calling (animals, body parts, and body parts of animals are particular favorites—bitch, ass, and horse's ass, for example).

It goes without saying that our secular society is no longer bent on protecting the name of God from "profane" use. But cultural mores, particularly in the conservative social environment of business, do continue to dictate that swear words and foul language indict the status, dignity, and sensibilities of the person to whom they are addressed. Swearing at an employee no longer implies anything about God, but certainly implies a great deal about the speaker's disrespect for and anger with the employee.

For that reason, foul language and swear words have been taken as prima facie evidence of verbal abuse, both in company discipline procedures and in court cases, insofar as they create and sustain a hostile work environment. But by identifying foul language as one prominent symptom of verbal abuse, we should not make the mistake of assuming that harsh and hurtful communications lacking foul language are not defined as verbal abuse. On average, in fact, most examples of verbal abuse in the workplace do not contain overt swear words or foul language—verbal abusers are too cagey to be caught in that easy trap. Instead, abusive language is much more likely to use negative comparisons ("you have the attention span of a flea") and rhetorical questions ("is anyone home inside your head?") to demean and persecute targeted victims.

Notice in all these uses of "inappropriate language" that the hot button word is chosen because it conflicts directly with some deeply held tenet or matter of taste for the audience. Saying "shit" in a prison causes no eyebrows to rise (we assume) because the term is so universally used there, and does not mark a deviation from the prevailing tastes or standards.

Similarly, the nature of the speaker, rather than the nature of the location, will sometimes dictate what terms can and can't be used. Black comedians such as Chris Rock and Eddie Murphy regularly use the word "nigger" in their routines, a term sure to bring swift action if used by a manager in an American corporation or by a government official at any level.

Chapter 5

A Step-by-Step Plan to Stop Verbal Abuse

Before enumerating proven techniques here and in Chapter 10 for stopping verbal abuse, we should ask a crucial question: Do you and your fellow employees *want* to put an end to this behavior? "But of course," someone may answer. "Who wouldn't want to call a halt to something as unpleasant and hurtful as verbal abuse?"

Ironically, one rueful answer to that question is "many marriages." Think, for example, of the couples you know who have spent years—decades, in some cases—engaged in day-to-day verbal combat, bickering their way through budgets, child raising, vacation planning, restaurant selection, sex, and salmon spread. Verbal abuse flows from husband to wife and back again, in a nonstop Ping-Pong game of verbal lashes. The question for such marriages or relationships generally is the same question we ask of verbal abuse in the workplace: Do they *want* to stop—and if not, why not?

Native good sense usually guides us to quit activities we don't like. If we try tennis and discover that we don't like it (or it doesn't like us), we give it up for another sport or pastime. We continue activities only if they bring us some form of fulfillment and pleasure, even at a subconscious level.

In the case of bickering couples, however, the freedom to vent one's frustrations over life's many annoyances with another person can become the fabric that binds a relationship together for life, as strange as that may seem. Here, verbal sparring becomes a form of interpersonal intimacy or familiarity, almost a strange expression of caring. One has only to think of television couples such as George Costanza's parents on *Seinfeld*, or the *Odd Couple*, to see the process at work.

Similarly in the workplace, the day-to-day melodrama that arises from verbal abuse may be the only thing that makes the workday interesting. When verbal abuse takes place, it immediately sets in motion a drama of bad guys and good guys, tormentors and victims. There's plenty to whisper about. The office has never been more alive or more interesting. Allegiances form and just as quickly change, with "whose side are you on" becoming the main concern of the day. We're all suddenly back in sixth grade again.

Like bickering marriages, some offices have lived with, and subtly encouraged, this caffeine diet of verbal abuse for months or years. The questions for those who work in the office are obvious: Do we want irascible old Mr. Phelps to give up his temper tantrums and bad moods? Doesn't it feel good (perversely so, perhaps) when Brenda gets yelled at for being so dumb? Don't we all spend our breaks buzzing about whether Allen will put in for a transfer due to his verbal run-in with his supervisor, and whether he will take Brett with him? Do we really want the boredom of peace and harmony, or would we prefer to stay with the *Sturm und Drang* of our verbal combat zone?

Employees who have recently been stung by verbal abuse probably have no difficulty answering such questions: "End verbal abuse now—it's hurting me and hurting the company!" But those who have positioned themselves on the sidelines, the voyeurs of verbal abuse upon others, may be less motivated to end an ongoing office spectacle that has produced its share of cruel enjoyment. The Romans, after all, cheered for the lions.

First, understand that no one (including the author of this book) can script precisely what you should say or do in the face of verbal abuse. These incidents always involve complicated variables—the personality of the abuser, your personality, the work circumstances, career risks involved, and so forth. Although you can load your quiver with well-designed arrows by reading this book and other works on verbal abuse, you alone can decide which arrows to shoot when verbal abuse occurs.

At the Moment of Verbal Abuse

Doctors speak of the "golden hour" of medical opportunity following a serious injury; if medical aid is not applied during that first hour, the patient's chances for recovery fall off dramatically. In the same way, we can propose the "golden minute" in incidents of verbal abuse. So much depends on what you do in that first minute, when it becomes obvious to you that verbal abuse is headed your way like a freight train.

Strategy One: Look the person in the eye, take a deep breath to gather your courage, and say (in your chosen words), "Stop. I'm willing to have this conversation, but I'm not willing to be shouted at" or, "have you swear at me," or "have you call me names."

Strategy Two: Again, look the person in the eye, take a deep breath, and say, "Time out. You're obviously not in control right now. Call me when we can have a rational conversation and I'll be glad to meet with you." Then leave without another word.

After an Incident of Verbal Abuse

Let's say that you are not able to prevent the incident. It may have happened too quickly for you to avoid, or you may have found yourself in a public setting (such as a meeting) where your response options were limited. As soon as possible after the incident of abuse, undertake one or more of the following strategies:

Strategy One: Write down exactly what was said to you, as best you can remember it, and what you said in response. The following recording card can be a helpful cue to pertinent categories of information, especially when your mind is reeling from the insult you have endured.

CONFIDENTIAL

Date:

Location of Incident:

Time of Incident (start and end times):

People Present:

Background Information:

My best memory of what was said by Party A (B, etc.):

My best memory of what I said:

Nonverbal or physical aspects of this incident:

What I did immediately after the incident:

Other details or follow-up information:

Writing down what happened has the double benefits of pinning down details before you forget them (as if you ever could?) and giving you a more distanced view of exactly what occurred. Wordsworth called the best poetry "emotion recollected in tranquility." The recording card is your opportunity to convert raw emotion into rational language.

Strategy Two: Take a long moment to check your own perceptions, using the *Five Signs* list in Chapter 1 as a guide. Face up in your own mind to any fuel you may have purposely or accidentally thrown on the fire of the incident at hand.

Strategy Three: Think through why you were singled out as the target of this abuse. Use the *Ten Reasons Why People Become Targets for Verbal Abuse* checklist in chapter 2 to help you with your self-analysis. (The goal here is not to blame yourself, but rather to discover whether the attack was purely personal, or instead was directed toward your position in the company or other factors.)

Strategy Four: Talk through the incident with a trusted friend. The operative word here is "trusted," because you will be telling this person your innermost feelings of anger, anxiety, and hurt, and you must rely on him or her not to pass your disclosure along to the company grapevine (where it can be distorted, amplified, and handed along as hot news to people you may not trust). It is important to have this talk with a friend not only to vent powerful emotions (and as a way to gain control over them), but also to invite this person's perspective on what you experienced. If your friend sees the incident in crucially different ways than you do, you have a strong impetus to reexamine your own perceptions, motives, and memories to make sure you are clear within yourself about the nature of the abusive incident.

Short-term Follow-up

Within a day or two of the incident, you should decide whether to devote your energies to receiving an apology, repairing the relationship, reporting the incident, clarifying information involved in the incident, or some mixture of these.

Strategy One: If you want to get an apology (certainly a good idea), don't pretend to continue with business as usual until you receive it. If the abuser does not volunteer the apology, take matters into your hands. In as unstressed a moment as possible, approach the person privately and say, "I feel that you owe me an apology." If the person balks or asks why, be prepared to tell them in detail why the apology is deserved. You can convey this information in a calm, noncombative way. He may refuse to give the apology, but you will feel stronger and more in control of the situation for having insisted on it. You gave them an opportunity to put things back on track.

Strategy Two: If you feel you can do without an apology and simply want to repair the relationship, arrange for a meeting with the person at a time when you both can relax into conversation without impending time commitments. If possible, have the meeting at some site other than where the abusive incident took place. (Meeting with the person at the scene of the accident, so to speak, may tend to bring back all the bad feelings associated with that occasion.) At this meeting tell how you felt about the treatment you received, and how you would like to be treated in the future. Be willing to listen to the other person's version of what they were "trying to say," even if it departs radically from what indeed was said. Pick up on phrases or ideas that seem conciliatory and build upon them.

Strategy Three: The abusive incident may have been so egregious (perhaps involving ugly name-calling, foul language, implied threats, and so forth) that you decide to report it through company channels to officers and administrators who can do something about the problem. As a general rule, it is better *not* to tell the verbal abuser about your plans ("I'm going to file a report with HR!") in advance of actually filing. Some offenders will beat a path to their superiors and to HR in an effort to explain away your complaint in advance. Be sure you know in detail how such complaints are handled within your company. If the company typically does nothing about claims of verbal abuse, you may want to put your efforts elsewhere (for example, in a conversation with your boss's boss) rather than working through grievance channels.

Strategy Four: Abusive incidents often involve a misunderstanding of key facts and figures. If you realize that the verbal abuser has incorrect information, you can make sure that the factual record is set straight in an e-mail clarification or personal meeting. Simply getting the facts straight is not a substitute for healing bruises in the relationship, but it may help the verbal abuser see the error of their ways.

Long-term Follow-up

Within a few days of the incident, make time to talk with the verbal abuser and communicate your expectations for future professional treatment and relations. Your goal should be to reach agreement on how the two of you will handle points of disagreement in the future.

If the person is unwilling to meet with you, or proves uncommunicative in the meeting, put down your thoughts in an even-tempered letter, with a copy saved to your files. (A blind copy to the person's boss can be considered, but these behind-the-back communications sometimes do more harm than good in establishing good working relations for the future.)

If you find that you are the target of retribution or continued abuse from the person, keep a log of what, when, where, how, and (if appropriate) why. Make some trusted third party aware of what's going on. Explore all your options within your company, including HR provisions for dealing with verbal abuse, union protections, and, if necessary, legal action.

Nipping Verbal Abuse in the Bud

To this point, we have focused primarily on how to recognize verbal abuse, and what to do about it when it happens. In actual business conversations, however, many potentially abusive situations can be headed-off at the pass, before they ripen into a full-blown problem. Notice in the following two dialogues how one speaker catches the first whiff of impending verbal abuse and steers the conversation in a more productive direction:

BOSS: Susan, I need to talk to you about these charts you've created.

SUSAN: Sure. Is there a problem?

BOSS: A problem? I would say so! Didn't you learn anything in college about—

SUSAN: (calmly, directly): Wait a second. Show me exactly what you don't like and I'll fix it.

BOSS: Well, for starters, this legend at the bottom of the chart is entirely too small to read when the chart is blown up onscreen. What were you thinking when—

SUSAN: No problem. I can double the font size right away. What else?

In this snippet (from an actual business conversation), Susan is successful in catching her boss before he launches into personal attacks about her education and intelligence. In a polite but firm way, she keeps redirecting the conversation back to the specifics at hand, with a focus on problem solving, rather than on blame or causes.

Here's another way to keep verbal abuse from popping out:

HEATHER (in a hostile tone): I heard you told the boss I was available for that trip to Cincinnati.

JOHN: You heard wrong. Do you want to know what I did tell the boss?

HEATHER (still angry): Don't play games, John. What did you say?

JOHN: Here's exactly what I said, "I can't go on the trip, but you may want to check with the rest of the team to see if anyone is available."

HEATHER: Did you think about asking me whether I wanted to go? That trip will totally screw up a ski weekend my boyfriend and I were going to take.

JOHN: It's the boss's decision whom to ask. I told him I couldn't go.

HEATHER: But you didn't suggest my name?

JOHN: Not at all. I wouldn't have done that without talking to you.

HEATHER: Well, I guess I got the wrong information. Sorry I jumped down your throat.

JOHN: No problem. I would have felt the same way. In the future, let's always check with each other before assuming the worst.

HEATHER: Good idea.

The key to preventing Heather's irritation from exploding into words she will regret lies in John's willingness to supply clarifying information. He doesn't take the bait of Heather's hostile tone by fighting fire with fire; instead, he calmly speaks to the issue that concerns her. Once she is convinced that John did not use her to accommodate his own needs and schedule, she settles down. Their relationship, in fact, may be stronger at the conclusion of this conversation for having worked through a problem successfully. Both commit to early communication about potential problems in the future.

Any management training seminar on verbal abuse can profitably spend some discussion time on practical ways to diffuse temperamental confrontations before blatant verbal abuse rears its head.

Ten Commandments for Managers and Supervisors Who Want to Avoid Verbal Abuse

I. Thou shalt not raise thy voice.

Commentary: No matter what the content, a raised voice instantly puts the other person on the defensive. His or her parry to your thrust sets a battle royal into motion. Verbal abuse is sure to ensue.

II. Thou shalt not swear.

Commentary: Just don't—not because the workplace is Sunday school, but because intelligent managers don't give their critics an easy charge to level.

...erson you are upset—but don't let those emotions break ...ut into behaviors such as verbal abuse that can damage ...ou and your prospects.

VII. Thou shalt focus thy criticism on the problem, not the person.

Commentary: If Richard miscalculated the budget figures, focus your attention on what he did wrong and why. Don't tread on the dangerous ice of Richard's personal qualities. (This includes disparaging remarks about his intelligence, commitment, or education.) You're trying to repair the problem, not assassinate the person.

VIII. Thou shalt not issue vague threats.

Commentary: If actual consequences will flow from the person's mistake, tell them so. But do not torment the person's imaginings with open threats such as "you'll be sorry," or "I wouldn't want to be in your shoes."

IX. Thou shalt not walk away while the other person is trying to explain.

Commentary: Turning your back on a person who is making an effort to explain a problem or situation is tantamount to "silent verbal abuse," or nonverbal abuse. If you feel you will explode with anger unless you get out of the person's presence, call a "time out" and arrange to meet later.

III. Thou shalt not call names.

Commentary: The use of derogatory na.
"Phony!" "Jerk!" and worse) are automatic "figh,
and prima facie evidence, if it comes to HR revie\
were guilty of verbal abuse.

**IV. Thou shalt listen more than thou speakes\
thou art upset.**

Commentary: Some people make you so mad that y\
are afraid of what you might say if you keep on talking. S\
be quiet. Use the sensation of bulging blood vessels in youi
temples as your signal to chill and listen.

V. Thou shalt not use sarcasm to wound others' feelings.

Commentary: Sarcasm (a mocking parody of what the
other person is saying) arouses the person's anger because
it is simultaneously patronizing and humiliating. Paraphrasing Shakespeare, speak with sincerity, and let who will be
clever.

**VI. Thou shalt tell others thou art upset without acting
upset.**

Commentary: Your employment contract does not
require that you leave your emotions at the door when
you enter company premises. Every good manager feels
strongly about the job and the work team. When you feel
angry emotions welling up inside, simply tell the other

X. Thou shalt hide the sword of thy anger because thou art smart.

Commentary: You don't get paid enough to get heart-pounding, vein-swelling mad at work. Your health, happiness, and professional image aren't enhanced at all by displays of rage. You're too smart to take the bait of all the people and circumstances that prod you toward anger.

Chapter 6

Understanding
Personality to Fight
Verbal Abuse

You may have noticed that you don't get along equally
well with everyone you meet. That's hardly news for any
of us. But you may have written off this common experience as "just chemistry," or "not my cup of tea." Leaving
personality connections in the mystery zone puts you one
step behind in your professional life.

The psychological theories of Swiss philosopher Carl Jung continue to provide an influential tool for interpersonal success in business. In 1921, Jung proposed the "type" theory—that is, the idea that each of us is predisposed to certain personality tendencies, which Jung arranged into four dimensions, with each dimension composed of opposite qualities. Some individuals, Jung said, are by nature more extroverted, some are more introverted. Some spend their energy handling details, while others work to grasp the big picture. Some operate predominantly by logic, some by emotion. Some are data gatherers, while others hurry on to conclusions.

You need to know "who you are" in this scheme of personality definition in order to predict and prepare for personalities quite unlike yours (in other words, people with whom you may experience conflict and verbal sparring).

The following instrument, originally printed in the book *Winning With Difficult People* (Barron's, 2004)[1], may help you understand your own basic personality tendencies. With these in mind, you can easily determine with which other personality types you are likely to bond or to clash. Verbal abuse often occurs when neither party sees a personality train wreck directly ahead. This short personality inventory can be your flashlight into the tunnel to at least spot the train and react accordingly before it reaches you.

Here's how this evaluation works. You simply enter your "a" or "b" choices on the scorecard at the end of the questions. The interpretive guide accompanying the scorecard will help you understand your scores and make applications to your business life.

Directions: Read each question and allow your "gut" response to guide your answer. In some cases, you may not have a strong preference, or neither of answers seems to be right for you. In all cases, choose the answer that comes closest to your opinion. (It may be most convenient to circle your answer ["a" or "b"] for each question, then transfer your answers to the scorecard when you have completed the test.)

1. In the workplace, do you prefer:

a. Making social conversation with many people during the day?
b. Making social conversation with only a few people during the day?

2. In learning a new work skill, do you prefer to be trained by:

a. Following a step-by-step set of instructions?
b. Grasping the big picture and trying your own approach?

3. Do your work associates value you most for:

a. What you think (that is, your rational abilities)?
b. What you feel (your "heart" or intuitions)?

4. As you review major accomplishments by others in your industry, do you believe their achievements have been due to:

a. Pushing hard to make things happen?
b. Looking beyond obvious answers for new possibilities?

5. In your work relationships, do you consider yourself:

a. Popular with many people?
b. Popular with only a few people?

6. In considering a job change, would you prefer to hear about:

a. What employees at a new company are doing?
b. How employees at the new company are being prepared for future challenges?

7. When a new worker enters your work environment, do you form impressions based on:

a. Their appearance and actions?
b. The way they make you feel when you are with them?

8. In making business purchases, do you select items:

a. Quickly, because you know what you want?
b. After careful comparison shopping?

9. At work do you prefer jobs that:

a. Bring you in contact with many people during the day?
b. Bring you in contact with few, if any, people during the day?

10. When you have too much to do in your day, do you respond by:

a. Finding extra energy to meet the challenges?
b. Stopping to revise your plans and schedules?

11. In managing others, would it be most important for you to be:

a. Logical?
b. Friendly?

12. In arranging business deals, would you tend to:

a. Save time for all concerned by spelling out the major points of agreement, and leaving minor points to good faith between the parties?
b. Spell out both major and minor details, even if such work takes extra time?

13. At work do you consider yourself to have:

a. Many friends?
b. Few if any friends?

14. Do you think a company leader should be:

a. Informative?
b. Organized?

15. When a coworker confides in you about a personal problem do you tend at first to:

a. Try to offer a possible solution?
b. Feel and express sympathy?

16. In superior/subordinate relationships at work, should duties between the parties be:

a. Stated clearly in written or spoken form?
b. Left open to allow for flexibility and new
   opportunities?

17. When meeting a new employee, do you tend to:

a. Take the initiative in showing warmth and friendliness?
b. Wait for him or her to show signs of friendliness?

18. Should children be raised to:

a. Learn real-world skills and behaviors as soon as
   they are ready?
b. Set goals and stick to their commitments?

19. In work relationships, is it more dangerous to show:

a. Too much emotion and personality?
b. Too little emotion and personality?

20. In designing interview questions for use in hiring a manager, would you tend to create:

a. Questions with definite answers?
b. Questions that are open-ended?

21. An old acquaintance (but not a good friend) unexpectedly encounters you in the lobby of a convention hotel. Do you tend to find this chance meeting:

a. Enjoyable?
b. Somewhat uncomfortable?

22. In choosing artwork to hang on company walls, would you tend to choose paintings that:

a. Are quite different from one another?
b. Work together to communicate a single theme or impression?

23. In deciding which candidate to support for a leadership position in your company, would you favor:

a. An intelligent, cool-headed candidate?
b. A passionate and well-intentioned candidate?

24. Do you prefer social get-togethers that are:

a. Carefully planned?
b. Largely unplanned?

25. In going out to lunch with coworkers, would you prefer to be with:

a. Many coworkers?
b. One or two coworkers?

26. Presidents of companies should have:

a. Excellent skills?
b. Well-developed plans?

27. You are passing through a city on business and want to stop by to say hello to a former colleague who lives there. Would you prefer to:

a. Make specific time and place arrangements with the person well in advance of your trip?
b. Give the person a pleasant surprise by "calling out of the blue"?

28. When attending a company social event taking place at 8 p.m., do you tend to:

a. Arrive right on time?
b. Arrive somewhat late?

29. In making business phone calls, do you:

a. Make the most of the conversation, allowing little time for the other person to speak?
b. Spend most of your time listening and commenting briefly on what the other person is saying?

30. In moments of leisure, would you prefer to read:

a. A letter to the editor in a news magazine?
b. An article about city planning?

31. In choosing movies, do you tend to select:

a. Movies that explain social conditions and historical periods?
b. Movies that produce laughter or tears?

32. In preparing to be interviewed for a job, do you think you should prepare to talk more about:

a. Your achievements?
b. Your future goals and plans?

33. If forced to accept dormitory accommodations during a conference, would you prefer to stay in a room:

a. With a few other compatible conference participants?
b. Alone?

34. In making work decisions, are you most influenced by:

a. The facts of the situation at hand?
b. The implications of the situation at hand?

35. In hiring employees to work for you, should they be primarily:

   a. Intelligent and wise?
   b. Loyal and hardworking?

36. In purchasing real estate, is it more important to:

   a. Be ready to snap up a good deal before it disappears?
   b. Have thorough knowledge of available properties?

37. In making a consumer complaint, would you prefer to:

   a. Call the company and talk to a customer representative?
   b. Write to the company?

38. When performing an ordinary work task, do you prefer to:

   a. Do whatever works?
   b. Do what is usually done?

39. In court, judges should:

   a. Follow the letter of the law.
   b. Show leniency or strictness where they think it appropriate.

40. When given a project to complete, would you prefer someone to give you:

a. A deadline?
b. The freedom to turn the project in when you feel it is ready?

41. When introducing two work associates who do not know each other, do you tend to:

a. Tell them each a bit of information about the other to facilitate conversation?
b. Let them make their own conversation?

42. Which is worse for a manager?:

a. To be too idealistic?
b. To be too flexible?

43. When you listen to a business presentation, do you prefer a speaker:

a. Who proves his or her points with data and specific examples?
b. Who communicates excitement and deep commitment for the topic?

44. At the end of the work day, do you spend more time thinking about:

a. What you did during the day?
b. What you are going to do the next day?

45. In planning your ideal vacation, would you choose a place where:

    a. You can meet with family and friends?
    b. You can be alone, or with only one to two family members or friends?

46. At work, which activity appeals to you more:

    a. Meeting deadlines?
    b. Predicting coming events?

47. Which would be more important to you if you were president of a company?

    a. That all employees understand their job responsibilities thoroughly.
    b. That all employees feel part of the company family.

48. As a member of a project team, would you prefer to be most involved in:

    a. The completion stage in which final details are wrapped up?
    b. The initial conceptualization stage in which approaches are debated?

49. In learning a new work skill, would you prefer to be taught:

    a. As part of a small class?
    b. One-on-one by a trainer?

50. If you had just two novels to choose between for leisure reading, would you be more likely to select:

a. A realistic novel about people and places?
b. A mystery novel at the end of which everything becomes clear?

51. When you consider your career path, do you believe you should:

a. Plan career moves months or years in advance?
b. Follow your heart as opportunities arise?

52. In paying tribute to a retiring company leader, should you focus primarily on:

a. The person's achievements?
b. The person's aspirations?

53. Do you think the main purpose of meetings in business is:

a. Getting to know one another and building team spirit?
b. Getting work done as efficiently as possible?

54. Are you most adept at:

a. Drawing conclusions from facts?
b. Raising long-term questions and issues?

55. The most important quality that a workforce can have is:

    a. An up-to-date education.
    b. Team spirit.

56. Which of the following words comes closest to describing your behavior at work?

    a. Impatient?
    b. Curious?

57. If your employer wanted to honor you at a luncheon, would you prefer a luncheon attended by?

    a. Many company employees?
    b. Your employer and one or two others?

58. In general, which quality has mattered more for highly successful companies:

    a. Common sense?
    b. Foresight?

59. If you had to choose, which of these two things would be better to say about a retiring employee:

    a. That he or she was smart at his or her job?
    b. That he or she cared deeply about coworkers?

60. In working on a team project, do you tend to:

a. Move it along to completion before the due date?
b. Make sure team members have considered all relevant information?

Scorecard

Transfer your answers and check in the appropriate spaces below.

1a ___ b___   2a ___ b___   3a ___ b___   4a ___ b ___

5a ___ b___   6a ___ b___   7a ___ b ___   8a ___ b ___

9a ___ b___   10a___ b___   11a___ b___   12a___ b___

13a___ b___   14a___ b___   15a___ b___   16a___ b___

17a___ b___   18a___ b___   19a___ b___   20a___ b___

21a___ b___   22a___ b___   23a___ b___   24a___ b___

25a___ b___   26a___ b___   27a___ b___   28a___ b___

29a___ b___   30a___ b___   31a___ b___   32a___ b___

33a___ b___   34a___ b___   35a___ b___   36a___ b___

37a___ b___   38a___ b___   39a___ b___   40a___ b___

41a___ b___   42a___ b___   43a___ b___   44a___ b___

45a___ b___   46a___ b___   47a___ b___   48a___ b___

49a___ b___   50a___ b___   51a___ b___   52a___ b___

53a___ b___   54a___ b___   55a___ b___   56a___ b___

57a___ b___   58a___ b___   59a___ b___   60a___ b___

___   ___   ___ ___   ___ ___   ___ ___ TOTAL
 M   S   J   P   T   E   C   R

Add up the total number of checks for the "a" and "b" columns. Then, for each pair of letters at the bottom of the columns, circle the letter for column containing the most checks. You should circle four letters all together. The letters refer to the eight personality descriptions presented below. The higher the number of checks, the more dominant that characteristic is in your personality.

Why four dominant traits? None of us consistently acts in accordance with only one personality characteristic. Instead, various traits (such as those you've identified by the letters you've circled) interact, often in unpredictable ways, to produce the whole personality known as "you."

Let's say, for example, that your score identifies you as a MJEC—with dominant traits in the Member, Juggler, Empathizer, and Closer categories. Read through the descriptions of these personality types and reflect upon how those traits interact in your personality. Perhaps in times of stress, one or more traits come to the fore. Perhaps some traits are more evident at home while others are dominant at work.

Personality Characteristics

M – Member

This personality trait predisposes you to enjoy and seek out the company of others. The Member joins groups willingly, finds ways to include others in activities, and may tend to avoid tasks that must be accomplished alone. The Member relies on the consensus of the group for important decisions, and may hesitate to form or express personal opinions without having them validated first by the group. The Member derives emotional support and strength from belonging, popularity, and having the respect of others.

S – Self

This personality trait predisposes you to individual initiation and solitary work habits. The Self joins groups only for a compelling reason, and even then only for the period of the task at hand. The Self looks with suspicion upon widely held opinions and groupthink. When faced by tasks too extensive or difficult for a single person to accomplish, the Self opts to divide work tasks into portions that can each be managed by an individual. The Self derives emotional support and strength from measuring up to personal standards, not the judgment of others.

J – Juggler

This personality trait predisposes you to minute-by-minute, seemingly practical adjustments to changing conditions. The Juggler manages to keep many tasks in progress at once, all in a partial state of completion. The panic of impending deadlines and the unpredictability of interruptions and emergencies are all energizing and challenging for the Juggler. It is a matter of pride to the Juggler that he or she can handle situations, cope, and eventually see projects through to fulfillment. The Juggler derives emotional support and strength from a sense of sustained busyness, as well as a conviction of his or her value to the group.

P – Planner

This personality trait predisposes you to place details, individual facts, and other data into patterns. The Planner then clings to these patterns tenaciously, for they serve to organize an otherwise bewildering array of discrete items. The Planner is resistant to receiving disorganized data before a plan has been developed; but after the planning stage, he or she welcomes information, particularly insofar as it supports the designated plan. The Planner derives emotional support and strength from a conviction of his or her usefulness in shaping disorderly projects and groups. To a degree, the Planner also derives emotional strength simply from the nature of the plan developed—its symmetry, scope, and interrelation of parts—no matter how events turn out.

T – Thinker

This personality trait disposes you toward finding, or attempting to find, logical links between thoughts, ideas, concepts, facts, details, and examples. The Thinker insists on postponing action until he or she "figures out" the underlying causes, effects, and relative accuracy or truth of propositions and assertions. When in a data gathering mode, the Thinker is intent on knowing more; but when in assimilating and ratiocinating modes, the Thinker may reject or postpone new input of any kind. The Thinker derives emotional support and strength from the satisfaction of reaching logically defensible solutions to problems. Whether anyone acts on the basis of those solutions is less important to the Thinker than the success of the mental processes involved in arriving at them.

E – Empathizer

This personality trait predisposes you to focus on the emotional content of situations, as experienced personally or by others. The Empathizer appraises new information or a new situation first according to its emotional potential: How do I feel about this? How do others feel? Who will be hurt? Who will be happy? The answers to these questions play a prominent role in shaping the Empathizer's eventual point of view and action regarding the new information or situation. The Empathizer derives emotional support and strength from his or her self-image as a sensitive, caring individual, and often from the gratitude and friendship of those targeted for his or her empathy.

C – Closer

This personality trait predisposes you to make conclusions, judgments, and decisive acts, sometimes contrary to established procedures and rules. The Closer is generally impatient with delays urged by others for additional thought, research, or planning. The Closer often grants that the whole truth is not known, but argues that enough of the truth is already available for adequate decision-making. This personality type can be deaf to input that does not contribute directly to finalizing projects and processes. The Closer derives emotional support and strength from his or her reputation in the group as an action-oriented, no-nonsense decision maker, and from the satisfaction of having used power, tolerance for risk, and a measure of daring to manage difficult problems and personalities.

R – Researcher

This personality trait predisposes you to postpone judgment and action so long as it is possible to acquire new information. The Researcher craves certainty and suspects conclusions reached without consideration of all the evidence. The Researcher frequently ignores both time and resource constraints in pressing on with the search for additional data. In communicating that data to others, the Researcher may not be able to successfully organize and summarize the data gathered, since these activities both involve the drawing of tentative conclusions. The Researcher derives emotional support and strength from the treasure hunt excitement of investigation, from the strong influence his or her findings have upon eventual planning, and from the admiration they receive from the group for being such a knowledgeable team member.

Using Personality Knowledge to Predict and Avoid Verbal Abuse

Much of our frustration with other people (and their frustration with us) stems not from any failure on behalf of either party, but instead on different perspectives, as suggested by the eight personality types discussed here. Imagine, for example, that a boss who is a Closer assigns an important project to a bright new employee who happens to be Researcher. Somewhere down the line as the deadline approaches, there is a good chance of verbal confrontation—and perhaps verbal abuse—as the Closer presses for completion of the project and the Researcher delves ever deeper into new sources of information. Here's a typical dialogue between a Closer and a Researcher to make the point:

CLOSER: Frank, we need to wrap that project up this afternoon.

RESEARCHER: This afternoon? I still have to run searches on two more search engines to make sure we haven't overlooked the latest information.

CLOSER: Frank, this could go on forever. The train is leaving the station. Let's get aboard!

RESEARCHER: Look, I just want the final product to be right. Give me another few days and we'll see where we stand.

CLOSER (losing patience): I know where we'll be standing—right here having this same discussion. Can you finish this up or do I have to bring in someone else?

RESEARCHER: That's fine with me. A new set of eyes will probably give us some new avenues for investigation.

You can understand why the Closer's blood pressure boils at this point. The Researcher, too, is feeling less than happy. He feels bullied by someone who doesn't appreciate his hard work as an investigator.

What could have been done in advance to avoid this confrontation? The boss, knowing he is a Closer, could have assigned another Closer in the company to work with Frank on the project. Or the boss could have passed over Frank entirely, knowing Frank's tendency to stretch work out until he had turned over every possible stone. Above all, the boss could have seen the problem coming and prepared for it, perhaps by building extra time into his schedule of deadlines. By evaluating personality differences at the outset, the boss could have virtually ensured that no last minute arguments or potential blowups would take place.

Let's consider one more example of "oil and water" personality types. The boss this time is a Self—a rugged individualist who is willing to go it alone against the current, and without the support of the crowd. Her executive assistant, Tom, is a Member: he is eager to know what's up with other workers and involved in most social aspects of company life. Their heated conversation goes like this:

BOSS: Tom, I need you to e-mail Barbara, Jill, and Allen. Let them know that they will be going on a quick business trip to Houston this weekend.

TOM (hesitating): I don't think Barbara is going to be too keen about that idea. She was planning a baby shower for her cousin on Saturday.

BOSS (sarcastically): How sweet. Just e-mail them.

TOM: And Jill's brother is home from college. They probably have planned something together.

BOSS: Look, Tom. We're running a business here. I don't care if their social life has to put on hold for a few days. I need them to go to Houston.

TOM: Maybe John and Richard would take their places?

BOSS (getting angry): What in the hell is going on? Do I have to send the e-mails myself?

TOM: I'm not trying to make you mad. I just know how Barbara and Jill are going to feel when they get my e-mail.

BOSS (firmly): Send the e-mail. If they have problems, tell them to see me! (She slams his office door)

Here we have the on-ramp to verbal confrontation and conflict not only between the boss and Tom, but also later one involving the boss, Barbara, and Jill. Incidents of verbal abuse don't drop from the sky, as if sprung from the brow of Zeus. They fester, grow, and finally explode—unless, of course, shrewd managers see them coming and find strategic ways to avoid them by using their knowledge of personalities.

The boss in this case might reason as follows: "I know that Barbara is a Juggler. If I explain that this trip is an emergency and I really need her to save the day, she will respond, no matter what her personal commitments. And I know Jill and Allen are both strong Thinkers. I'll put them onto the project of getting a PowerPoint presentation ready for the Houston people. They won't mind the trip if they're doing something they like to do. Since Tom feels bad for these employees and doesn't want to take the heat himself from their upset feelings, I'll have him prepare an e-mail and send it out under my name, not his."

These little accommodations to the easy route, rather than the rocky road, make business process flow more smoothly and help employees work together less stress-fully. The alternative is treating people as if you were a kid with a chemistry set—throwing chemicals together without a thought for what might happen. Explosions in the form of verbal conflict and abuse are often the result of a manager's failure to think about his or her own personality tendencies, and those in the work group.

Chapter 7

Five Hard Pieces: Scenarios of Verbal Abuse

If a picture is worth a thousand words, a scenario has to be worth at least five hundred words in its ability to depict complex relationships and real-world problems. In the following scenes, employees experience personal and professional distress from a verbal encounter with a boss, coworker, or client. After each scenario, we will discuss whether the encounter did, in fact, constitute verbal abuse. In that discussion, we will speculate on:

- What was apparently going on inside the head of the verbal abuser?

- Why the person targeted for abuse was selected?

- Whether the person's response to abuse was effective or ineffective?

- How the situation was finally resolved?

You can make the best use of these scenarios by posing these four questions to yourself as you read each case. See if you agree or disagree with the ensuing discussion.

Scenario One: He Screamed at Me

Evelyn S. had worked at Tribune Industries as a midlevel account executive for the last five years and had a reputation for steady, if uninspired, work. She had a few friends at work, but tended to keep to herself. She rarely spoke up at meetings unless asked a direct question. Evelyn required careful direction for each project she undertook. She tended to work independently and preferred to have few interruptions.

Evelyn's last project involved the composition of a major report on the market possibilities for Elastoplex, a new Tribune product for home insulation during the construction phase. Through no fault of Evelyn's, the new product was running somewhat late to market. Winter was approaching, and with it a slowdown in home construction and remodeling. Evelyn's boss did not want to approve a sizable budget for marketing the product until he had Evelyn's report about marketing conditions. He started calling her every morning to ask when she would be done with her work. His tone had grown increasingly impatient, not so much out of frustration with Evelyn, but with the whole Elastoplex mess. His neck was on the block if this expensive project didn't get to market, and successfully so, in the near future.

Typical of her work style, Evelyn informed her boss that she is making progress and would be done exactly on the date the report is due, but not a moment sooner.

On the due date and time, Thursday at 11 a.m., Evelyn walked into her boss's office and handed him her thick, well-documented report. He thanked her and she went back to her desk.

Twenty minutes later Evelyn's boss phoned her: "Evelyn, I need to talk with you right away." She entered her boss's office to see him red faced, with her report pages spread out helter skelter across his desk. "Evelyn," he yelled, "what in the hell is this? I specifically told you to develop a report on how Elastoplex would fare in today's market. This is just a report on home insulation products. There's very little in here at all about Elastoplex. Jesus Christ, Evelyn!"

Evelyn was taken aback by her boss's angry tone. She knew he had a temper, but she never expected to be the target of his rage. She tried to explain herself: "You told me to develop a report on the markets that Elastoplex would be entering. That's what I did."

"Damn it, Evelyn," her boss continued to shout, closing his door now so that no one else would hear, "you've spent two weeks of company time and money putting together a bunch of pages we can't even use. For god's sake, didn't it occur to you that we would be making budget decisions based on your report? How can we decide any-thing when there's nothing here about how Elastoplex would do against its competitors?"

Evelyn felt her cheeks growing hot and her heart beat-ing fast. "I guess I misunderstood the assignment," she said weakly. Her emotions were welling up inside. "I tried my best to...to..." She couldn't help herself. She burst into sobs, unable to speak further. Her boss shoved a box of tissues at her and walked out of his own office, leaving Evelyn standing there in tears.

What's Going on Here?

Here we have a classic case of the "quiet mouse and the roaring lion." They have no particular problems work-ing together until a crisis occurs. Then all that's worst about each of them—Evelyn's timidity and her boss's ferocity—comes out in one cataclysmic, destructive incident. Given Evelyn's obsessive concern to dot all her i's and cross all her t's at work, she was devastated not only by the fact that her boss rejected her work, but that he did so in a rage that frightened her to her core. She would remember this awful day the rest of her life. It's doubtful that she would ever "come back" from the incident as a productive employee. If she remained in her present job, she would second guess everything she did.

The *Evelyns* of work life often find themselves em-ployed by strong, temperamental bosses. They gravitate toward individuals who seem to have a firm grip on the wheel and an unswerving sense of direction. To some degree they see strong bosses as their protectors. On the flip side, this kind of employer seeks out easy to manage, somewhat frightened, personalities who are under the boss's complete control. It doesn't take more than an occasional growl or fist pounded on the table to send shivers through this kind of workforce.

From the perspective of Evelyn's boss, the incident was hardly remarkable. "I just got mad," he said. "My employees know that I have a temper and most of the time they don't push me too far. But Evelyn's mistake made me livid."

Evelyn's boss certainly didn't see his tirade as verbal abuse, but simply as an amplified version of the management style—Management by Getting Mad—that he used every day to maintain control of his employees.

Evelyn's tears, although understandable, were an ineffective way to respond to her boss's verbal explosion. Her boss took her tears as a tacit admission of her mistake—"she knew she blew it and just started crying"—and ended their encounter by walking out. In the days following this traumatic moment, Evelyn kicked herself many times for breaking down in tears. She wondered how things could have gone differently if the conversation had continued, the boss had calmed down, and she'd had the opportunity to explain in detail why she developed the report as she did.

The aftermath: Evelyn's boss never apologized for his outburst. Elastoplex eventually came to market with mediocre results, for which Evelyn's boss privately blamed her. Evelyn took on minor work assignments in the months after the blowup, but due to recurring headaches and sleeplessness found she was taking more and more sick days. She resigned from her job a month ago and was living off her savings while she tried to get her spirits up to interview for a new job somewhere else, preferably where bosses wouldn't yell at her.

Did verbal abuse take place? Some would argue that this expression of rage on the boss's part was a one-time only incident and therefore did not qualify as verbal abuse. Bosses, they would claim, are human and have a right to blow up once in a while. The counterargument is that the severity of the boss's reprimand was so far beyond his usual style with employees that it did indeed constitute verbal abuse. When repetition of verbally abusive incidents is not present, we look to the intensity of a single event to decide whether verbal abuse took place. Certainly from Evelyn's point of view, she was verbally abused, with crippling personal and professional results.

What could Evelyn have done? She has played this incident over and over in her mind during the months since. She wishes she had called a "time out" at her boss's first sign of rage and his first use of expletives. She could have firmly and calmly told her boss that she would be glad to come back to his office when he calmed down. If he insisted that she "shut up and sit down," she could have repeated her offer to come back when he was in control of his temper. Until that time, she wasn't going to talk with him because she would not be yelled at by anyone, including her boss. It's possible, of course, that if Evelyn had taken this course of action, her boss would have screamed, "You're fired!" But he would then be in the embarrassing position of having to explain to his superiors in the company why he fired an employee who had offered to talk out their problems once he had calmed down.

Scenario Two: The Insulting Client

Francisco O. was 61 years old and handled product distribution for a wide variety of clients in the electronics industry. The company he worked for, Morgan Ditribution Network (MDN), located smaller manufacturers who do not have their own sales forces. MDN then assigned one of its account executives, like Francisco, to work closely with the client to find the best possible channels of distribution for their product.

Francisco had a potential client, Bob Johnson Enterprises, which manufactured circuit board testing equipment. The founder and company president, Bob Johnson, wanted to interview Francisco before signing on as an MDN client. At that interview, the following conversation ensued:

JOHNSON: Your last name is Ortega?

FRANCISCO: That's right.

JOHNSON: Not many Mexicans in my business.

FRANCISCO: Actually there are more than you think. Mexican-Americans make up about 30 percent of the workforce in the electronics field here in California.

JOHNSON: No, I'm talking about managers. So, Ortega, you're still playing in a young man's game.

FRANCISCO: Feel free to call me Francisco. A young man's game?

JOHNSON: I mean I just don't see many grey heads out there in the electronics business. My average employee is 29 years old. I'm only 42 years old myself.

FRANCISCO: Let me give you a quick sketch of what MDN can do for your product line.

JOHNSON: Hold on, Ortega. I'm still trying to get a picture of you selling our product to young, Anglo retailers.

FRANCISCO: What bothers you about that picture?

JOHNSON: You're just not the image that comes to mind when I think about the representation I want for my company. It's a big step for us to sign over distribution rights, and we want to make sure the fit is right.

FRANCISCO: The fit? MDN has a strong sales record, and my own track record is—

JOHNSON: Yeah, yeah. But I'm talking about image. No salesman your age calls on me. And nothing against Mexicans, but you know how it is.

FRANCISCO: What do you mean?

JOHNSON: It's a fast track and young chargers—you know, your computer-jock type—are the only ones with credibility.

FRANCISCO: All I can say is that we have a lot to offer you at MDN. I can show you figures from several of our past accounts.

JOHNSON: Like I said, we were looking for something else in terms of our representation. But thanks for stopping by.

What's Going on Here?

Francisco Ortega had no doubts about his ability to represent his clients successfully. During his three decades in the electronics business, he built up an enviable network of contacts, and a track record that any salesperson would be proud of. But in his initial interview with Bob Johnson, he ran up against the stone wall of ageism and racism. Francisco had prepared himself thoroughly to speak about virtually any business issue the client brings up. He was not prepared to deal with the nonbusiness flack that Johnson throws his way.

Here was a case of prejudice outside the bounds of usual legal protections. Had this same conversation taken place in a job interview, Francisco would have been the first to protest that his rights were being violated by making his age and race an issue in the employment decision.

Bob Johnson, however, was not his employer. Johnson did not hesitate to throw his weight around as a potential client. He pictured himself as "one up" due to the business he can have given to Francisco; he viewed Francisco as "one down" due to his need for Johnson's account.

The verbal abuse that occurred in this interview was not accompanied by anger (although Francisco no doubt felt his temperature rise as Johnson pressed on with comments about Francisco's age and ethnicity). Here the abuse was located in the content of the communication, not its manner of delivery. Johnson was outwardly civil in the way he spoke to Francisco, but abusive in his denigration of Francisco as a person and a professional.

What could Francisco have done? As a salesperson, Francisco developed a high tolerance level over the years for the bluster and blather fed to him by many potential clients. He had listened patiently as clients brag about their companies, products, and prospects. In this case, however, Francisco's tolerance and patience did not serve him well as Johnson veered into unexpected and prejudicial territory.

Walking away from Johnson's office, Francisco thought about what he could have done and said. One option was to stop the conversation at the first sign of prejudice on

Johnson's part: "Mr. Johnson, I'm experienced and successful at what I do. But if age is your main criteria for this account, I don't think we have much else to talk about." That option would have felt good for Francisco, who rankled when he thought back to Johnson's smug and biased comments about "a young man's game." But stopping potential clients short has never been part of Francisco's sales strategy.

Another option, one that Francisco resisted, would have been to defend who he is to a bigot. "I'm not going to lower myself to his level by trying to explain that people in their 60s can do the job for him, or that Mexican-Americans never have to apologize for their culture or ethnicity," he said to himself. "Prejudice is [Johnson's] problem and I'm not going to be the one to straighten him out."

A final option—the one Francisco wished he had taken—would have been to counter Johnson's closet prejudice by throwing open the doors. Specifically, Francisco could have arranged a second meeting that included his company's vice president for sales. The gambit here would be to stifle verbal abuse by raising its visibility rather than by educating its source. Johnson, after all, was using the privacy of his office and his one-on-one conversation with Francisco to say things that he probably would not say if others were present. The vice president would have been ideally positioned to speak to Francisco's excellent track record and contacts in the industry. By bringing in other observers, Johnson would have been forced back on track to business issues, rather than allowed to stray into verbally abusive areas of bias.

Scenario Three: Meeting Mayhem

Wendy Liu liked her title and responsibilities as Team Leader of an eight-person team tasked with proposing a menu of cafeteria benefits for a large food services company. Her team had met every few days to discuss the wide range of possible benefits for employees and to prioritize the most desirable of these benefits.

Wendy's leadership style had been purposely nondirective. She wanted each member of her team to be an independent thinker and to resist pressures to conform to popular opinion. As a result, the final proposal from her team was a bit late—but Wendy felt the week or two of extra meetings were well worth the rich thinking and wide ranging discussions that now took place when her team got together.

The team's eventual proposal, probably a week or so away, would be much better for the additional time they had taken. Several team members had told Wendy that they had never enjoyed working so much on a team before. One member said, "You've made us feel that we are each in charge of the team. The meetings are actually fun. We forget sometimes who is the Team Leader, and that's a good thing."

With the good feelings radiating from her team, Wendy didn't feel concerned when her boss rather suddenly called the entire team in for a 2 p.m. meeting. He must have some new input, she reasoned. When she entered the meeting room, however, she could tell by her boss's face and distant manner that "something was up."

Indeed it was. Wendy's boss opened the meeting with the following diatribe: "I brought you all together to tell you how disappointed I am in the way you've conducted yourselves over the past several weeks. I invested a lot of salaried time in putting eight of you on a team and I expected a final report from you by now. Now I understand that you're still a week away from finishing."

Wendy tried to break in, but was harshly silenced by her boss. "Not now, Wendy. I hold you largely responsible for these delays. You clearly don't know what it means to be a Team Leader. You don't just get people together and let them talk. From what I can tell, your team meetings have basically been long coffee breaks."

Again Wendy tried to interrupt.

"Damn it, Wendy, I don't want to hear excuses," her boss continued. "You didn't structure the meeting time, you didn't have firm agendas, and it's no wonder that you don't have your work done on time. You weren't a business leader for this team—you were just a cheerleader."

"I resent that," Wendy blurted out. She waited for other team members to speak up in her defense, but they were frozen to their chairs as the boss glared around the room.

"Screw your resentment!" the boss hissed. "I'm getting pressure from the Executive Committee for a final proposal and now I discover that no one has been driving the bus on your team. You can resent criticism all you want, Wendy, but the plain fact is that you've let me down, and you've let your team down, by not doing your job. I'm bringing Gene Evans in to take your place and I expect that proposal on my desk by close of business tomorrow."

The meeting ended on that sour note. One by one team members came to Wendy to tell her how unfair the boss had been. They told her again what a great team leader she had been and how they would miss her meetings. Thoroughly shocked and discouraged, Wendy smiled weakly and thanked them for their support. She wished she had heard some of that support at the meeting.

What's Going on Here?

Wendy was ambushed with a brutal tongue-lashing by her boss, replete with profanity, in front of her peers. Her attempts to speak up on her own behalf were put down by his bullying rant. The boss purposely chose a public occasion (the meeting), rather than a private conference, for his devastating criticism. He arranged the circumstances to maximize embarrassment for Wendy. By directing his withering blast at the team leader, he dared any other team member to speak up in her defense. They knew they would get the same verbal treatment.

Unbeknownst to Wendy, her boss was practicing "pass along" verbal abuse. Only hours before, he had been the victim of an equally brutal dressing-down by his superiors in the company. They wanted to wrap up the cafeteria benefits matter "yesterday," and tore into her boss for not producing an acceptable proposal on time. Still stinging from that confrontation, he had called together Wendy and her team to "pay forward" the pain—he wasn't going to be the only one taking the heat on this issue.

Later, Wendy sat at her desk thinking through what had happened and what she could have done. She had been reduced to silence by her boss's belligerence. Anything she said would only have increased his rage.

She tried to make sense out of the horrific incident by sifting out fact from fiction. It was a fact, she admitted to herself, that the project had run past its deadline. But this was not unusual, she knew, for team projects in the company, and her boss certainly had not bugged her about the deadline. It was also true, she granted, that her team meetings were looser in structure than meetings conducted by other company leaders. What was not true, however, was the boss's accusation that she had no agenda in mind. Wendy knew that she was simply trying to coax the best insights out of each team member by giving them the freedom to express themselves.

The aftermath: Wendy resolved never to take a leadership role in the company again. In the future, she would do the work assigned to her and not risk any creative contributions. She would also start sending her resume around. She didn't want to work for her boss one day longer than necessary.

What could Wendy have done? Without making excuses for her boss's bullying and punishing behavior in the meeting, we can imagine how things would have gone differently had Wendy kept information flowing to her boss throughout her time as team leader. In this case, big explosions can be prevented by a series of "pressure release" points. Before the deadline, Wendy could have let her boss know that the team was requesting extra time to fully develop their rich insights. If the boss objected, at least that resistance would have been communicated civilly (probably by e-mail). During the period after the deadline had elapsed, Wendy could have kept up her progress reports to the boss as a way of sensing how much "leash" she had to complete her work.

This option in no way lessens the boss's foolish choice to verbally abuse Wendy in front of her team. We can see, however, that big blowups can often be circumvented by keeping updates flowing and dealing with the minor "pinch points" as they occur.

Scenario Four: Late to the Party

Brad E. was still in his probationary period as an entry level accountant for a nationwide chain of department stores. He found the work interesting, but the regimen of getting to work at 8 a.m. was still a stressor for him—certainly a different lifestyle than his last couple years at the fraternity house. In his first month on the job, Brad had been about half an hour late to work on three occasions, once due to traffic problems, and the other two times due to late night partying.

His immediate supervisor, Todd, had been cool about these slight infractions of the work rules. But Todd's boss, Martha, had noticed Brad's late arrivals on a timesheet. The "Iron Lady," as she was not too affectionately known in the office, made it her personal mission to remind all new employees of the importance of getting to work on time.

Last Tuesday, in spite of his best efforts to get himself up and out of bed, Brad blew into the office at 8:35. Standing at the door was Martha. "Your name is Brad, isn't it?" she asked.

"Yes, and I know I'm a bit late," he responded. "My car wouldn't start and I had to call AAA, but they had two calls ahead of me. It wasn't my fault."

After taking a deep breath, Martha continued.

"Brad, I'm aware of your arrival times so far in your probationary period," she said. "I don't know whether to believe you or not about the car problem. I suppose I could call AAA to see if they answered a call to your address. But let's leave things this way: I'm giving you your last notice about late arrivals. If you arrive late again, you won't get my recommendation for continued employment. If a real emergency occurs, call me personally at the moment to let me know what's happened and how I can verify it. We're serious about beginning business at 8 a.m. here."

Brad looked at her in disbelief. "Yeah, okay, I get the point." He turned on his heel and walked to his office to stew over this lecture from the Iron Lady.

An hour later Brad knocked on Todd's door.

"Do you have a minute?" Brad asked. "Something happened this morning that I think was really unfair and downright abusive. I don't know whether to go to HR with it or not, especially since I'm still on probation." Todd settled back to listen to Brad's version of the story.

"I told her about my car problems and she had the nerve to say she didn't know whether she believed me. She even said she might call AAA to check up on me! I think that's abusive."

Todd interrupted to ask whether Brad's car problems were real or invented.

Brad rubbed his hand across his forehead. "Well, I had to say something—I mean, it's my fourth time being late. But that's not the point. You don't threaten to investigate when someone gives you a reasonable excuse. She's basically calling me a liar! And she says she wants me to call her personally if I have another emergency. I'm not going to take this kind of verbal abuse from anyone, even if she is the big cheese."

What's Going on Here?

Clearly, Martha spoke directly to Brad in a manner that could hardly be called friendly. She chose her words carefully: in fact, she never called him a liar (although he had lied); she speculated about checking out his story, but did not say she would do so; and she set out a specific plan for Brad in case he experienced a real emergency that made him late in the future.

Brad felt belittled by the whole experience. "She talked to me as if I were still in high school and had skipped class," he told Todd. "I'm a professional here and I expect to be treated that way."

Todd wisely recommended that Brad not file any complaint against Martha with HR. He explained as follows: "Brad, you got your feelings hurt by Martha's way of speaking to you. But your irritation doesn't mean that she verbally abused you. Probably if I had been standing at the door, we would have had a friendlier conversation about your late arrival. Martha has a different style: she tells it like it is, and lets the chips fall where they may. It would be another matter if she screamed or swore at you. She didn't."

Todd was correct. No verbal abuse took place in Martha's strict admonishment to Brad. As his employer, she had every right to evaluate the veracity of his claims and to warn him about future infractions of the work rules. Employers are not under any obligation to relate to employees in a friendly manner (although such relations are usually desirable). Nor do their words have to be expressed in a way that employees find pleasing. If Brad wanted to avoid further unpleasant encounters with Martha, he would well-advised to get to work on time. That outcome was no doubt what she had in mind when she chose to speak to him sternly, but not abusively.

Scenario Five: But You Said

Lincoln P., a general manager of a large upscale audio and video store, wondered why Christine, one of his marketing managers, looked upset as she entered his office. Just at the point of tears, she quickly told her story.

"My husband and I are thinking about buying our first house," she explained. "It's a lot of money and we don't have much margin for making a mistake. I heard by the grapevine that layoffs might be coming in the next few months. I need to know if they are and, if so, if I'm on the list before we plunge into this major financial decision to buy a house. If I don't have a job, we wouldn't be able to make the mortgage payment. We would probably lose everything."

"Nope," Lincoln replied breezily. "I know nothing definitive about layoffs. As far as I know, we're doing pretty well as a company and the big bosses in Chicago want everyone to keep their noses to the grindstone. Rumors about layoffs just cause people to quit caring and quit working. That's the last thing we need if we're going to hit our sales goals for this quarter."

"So I can move ahead with this house thing?" Christine asked directly.

"There aren't any guarantees in life, Christine," Lincoln said with a smile. "But I haven't been notified of decision to start laying off employees."

During the next week, Christine and her husband plunked down their small nest egg as the down payment on their first house together. The following Friday, Christine took her friend Jill to lunch to celebrate.

"The house is just what we've been dreaming about," Christine gushed. "I can't wait for you to see it."

As Jill looked at her Christine's smile faded.

"What's wrong?" Christine asked.

Jill spoke slowly and quietly. "I don't know for sure, Christine, but I saw some copies of memos from last month when I was filing for Lincoln. There were two or three different proposals for laying off employees here. Your name was on two of the plans and my name was on one. I don't want to bring you down, but I had to tell you. Didn't you check with Lincoln before getting into this house deal?"

What's Going on Here?

Words can be abused, and people can be appallingly hurt by those words, without a single swear word or a raised voice. In fact, the verbal abuse in this case was delivered with a smile. Lincoln, whose bonus depended upon his making quarterly numbers, had strong motive for, as he said, "keeping [everyone's] nose to the grindstone." Technically, he had not been informed of any "decision" to lay people off. But he was certainly well-aware that layoffs were coming in one form or another, and he may have even been aware of (or responsible for) the appearance of Christine's name on two of the layoff proposals.

Lying, or letting language stray far from integrity through a technicality, is one form of verbal abuse that

gets little press, but a lot of practice, in American companies. We often "manage by mystery," leaving employees in
a fog of half-truths, misinformation, and disinformation.
Because these employees are never privy to what managers
actually knew, these managers can always escape the accusation of lying by claiming that they too were in the dark.

Admittedly, there are times in business when a manager cannot reveal everything he or she knows about company plans or prospects to subordinates. For example,
salary offers for new hires are not typically shared with
seasoned employees, who may be earning quite close to
the same amount. But saying truthfully, "I can't say," is
better than pretending not to know.

Although no one has tallied their number with any pre-
cision, it would be fair to guess that incidents of workplace
verbal abuse in the form of lies far outnumber incidents of
verbal abuse characterized by anger, swearing, and name-
calling. Further, it's safe to guess that quiet lies prove much
more damaging to relationships and careers than do noisy
verbal blowups.

The act of verbal abuse poses real risks to the abuser.
He or she can get in trouble in the company in large and
small ways if caught delivering blatant verbal abuse. Therefore, most verbal abusers have become adept at subtly using
harmful words, always teasing at the margins of what is
acceptable and what is abusive. Action against verbal abusers, in fact, is often delayed for months or years because
of this ambiguity—"did he say what I thought he said?"
And the verbal abuser prolongs such delay by statements
such as "That's not what I said—and certainly not what I
meant!" when confronted by evidence of verbal abuse. In
many companies, verbal abuse becomes a game of sorts,
with the art of the sport lying in causing emotional and
professional death by a thousand tiny cuts instead of one
major, obvious thrust.

Eleven Additional Voices From Victims of Verbal Abuse

If you find yourself in the limbo of suffering from what seems to be verbal abuse, but not being able to put your finger precisely on the inappropriate nature of what is being said to you, use this additional list of first person recollections from victims to help you recognize the unwelcome presence of verbal abuse in your workplace, and perhaps right across your desk.

1. *"I am being singled out for harsh, unnecessary language that is not used on my peers."* The language at hand does not have to be filled with swear words, nor does it have to be delivered at the top of the boss's lungs. The point here is that you alone are targeted for a type and intensity of hard language, even if it is said in a low hiss out of the hearing of others.

Example (boss to employee, in a quietly angry voice): "You listen to me and listen to me good. If you want to disagree with me a meeting, you tell me after the meeting. You got it or are we going to have this little conversation again?"

2. *"I am referred to by inappropriate nicknames and epithets that undercut my professionalism and insult my dignity as a person."* Nicknames, even when intended by the boss or others as terms of endearment, aren't endearing when they make people feel diminished, ridiculed, or absurd. Similarly, inappropriate phrases constitute verbal abuse when

they communicate attributions that harm a person's professional reputation or viability.

Example (supervisor to subordinates Brenda and Bill): "Bill, I'm going to send Foxy here along with you on this sales call. If the guy doesn't fall in love with our product, maybe he will at least fall in love with Brenda."

3. *"The same message is repeated so often that it seems like punishment. I get the message. Why do I have to hear it over and over?"* Hitting people over the head with the same verbal onslaught quickly exhausts their patience and wears upon their sense of self-respect. Workers should not have to submit to the same verbal tactics used on hard-to-train dogs, let's say, where constant repetition may be the only way to change behavior.

Example: (team leader to team member): "I've said this to you a dozen times before and I'll say it a dozen times again, if I have to, every time we meet. John, there is no 'I' in 'TEAM.' Do you get it? There is no 'I' in 'TEAM.' Say it with me: There is no 'I' in 'TEAM.'"

4. *"I hear more foul language at work than I ever hear on the street. Sometimes these words are said directly to me and sometimes I just hear them as part of the way people talk in this office. I'm no purist, but I am offended by the type and frequency of foul language used all around me at work."* At the headquarters of a large San Francisco insurance company, the boss decided the display in the office halls what he conceived to be cutting edge photographs from a traveling photo exhibit. The black

and white photos were stark images of roadkill. Without challenging the boss's concept of art, workers in the company quickly let it be known that they would not show up at their offices so long as they were surrounded by vivid images of animal suffering, no matter what the reputation of artist/photographer. In the same way, workers without apology can object to a work environment filled with verbal displays of crude, unsavory terms and phrases.

Example: (manager in a weekly meeting): "I say fuck the forecasts and full speed ahead. I'm pissed off at these sons of bitches who think they can twiddle with math on their computers and derail a goddamn project we have busted our butts on, for Christ's sake."

5. *"I am the target of language that includes vague threats about some kind of harm to me in the future."* Verbal abusers often like to drive home their attack more by what they don't say, or say between the lines, rather than what they do say. This *implied verbal abuse* makes use of innuendo, half-statements, and suggestion to rouse doubt, anxiety, and downright terror in the minds of the verbally abused. Because the threat is open-ended, the threatened person does not know whether he or she risks some kind of future retribution at work, or some out of the workplace vengeance, such as slashed tires or other physical violence. We tend to imagine—and fear—the worst alternatives among the possibilities suggested by the verbal abuser.

Example: (one division head to another, both competing for resources in the company): "If you buck me on this or go behind my back, all I can say is that you may win the battle in the short run. But you'd better watch your back. You've heard of karma? You'll be earning bad karma with me, buddy, and I'm an enemy you don't want to have. You can win a battle but lose the war—big time, you know what I mean?"

6. *"My boss chooses to humiliate me publicly when he could have spoken to me privately about the problem at hand."* Bosses, those most human of all human beings, don't always choose the right time and place for words of criticism or admonishment. But every worker senses when a boss or supervisor repeatedly goes out of his or her way to ratchet up the "embarrassment factor" as part of negative words. The effect is not unlike the old Puritan practice of placing the "sinner" in wooden stocks and bracketing their head and hands, so that public ridicule could be heaped on the misdoer. Although stocks are now out of fashion, the public venues of meetings certainly are not. Some verbally abusive bosses choose meetings as an occasion for what one author has called "drama and trauma"—the blessing of the saints and the whipping of the slaves.

Example (boss, leading a meeting): "Thanks for that update on your project, Bob. Before we move on, I want to tell you that was the sloppiest job of reporting I have heard in all my years at this company. Either you didn't spend enough time preparing, or you're functionally illiterate. Your PowerPoint slides were a mess and you spoke as if you were at a funeral, not near the kickoff for a new product line. If I had to give you a grade, Bob, it would be an F, maybe with a minus sign in front of it."

7. *"I hate it when people use language that attacks what I am, not what I do. That's verbal abuse."* Too true. When we sign on as employees in any company or organization, we expect that our actions there will be fair game for legitimate criticism. If we go over budget, for example, we expect to hear about our mistake from our manager or director. But criticism of our actions is quite different from criticism of our character or nature. Nothing in our employment contract allowed for attacks aimed at the core of our being, including our personalities and individual dignity.

Example (coworker to coworker): "God, how can you live with yourself? You're so fucking passive, like a stamp machine at the post office, just grinding away. Don't you have any ambition? I'm getting out of this job as soon as I can, but you're going to be here forever."

8. *"I am verbally abused at work by language that refers to my ethnicity, age, gender, religion, and physical shape. I'm glad I'm not a person with handicaps—they would probably mock that, too."* In spite of ubiquitous HR training sessions on what managers can and can't make reference to, the sad fact is that American workplaces are rife with discriminatory language, sometimes said to workers' faces, but more often whispered behind their backs. Because the overt use of such language (let's say, in hiring interviews or performance evaluations) often lands the company in court, too many managers have learned to play the race, gender, age cards more subtly, usually without witnesses to confirm the incident of verbal abuse. Coworkers and subordinates are just as guilty, using discriminatory language as the "punch line" in criticism of their bosses.

Example (manager to a Hispanic female subordinate): "You're doing the mother thing too much with your group, Alice. Even if it's not part of your culture, you've got to take charge and whip them into shape. You're old enough to be their grandmother, for god's sake, and they still walk all over you."

Additional Example (subordinate to others, speaking about supervisor): "He's fat, man. Have you seen him at lunch? It's like steam shovels with both hands, packing in the food. Next time we have a meeting I'm going to get in there early to put two chairs right next to each other where he usually sits. It's going to take two chairs to hold his fat ass pretty soon. Tell everybody about the two chairs. It will be funny. He won't know why we're laughing at the meeting."

9. *"The kind of verbal abuse I most dislike is my boss's fairy-tale version of how others feel about me."* Some religions to this day practice social ostracizing, in which a person guilty of some infraction is physically shunned by everyone else in the community. If he or she is walking down one side of the street, members of the religion will make it a point to cross so they walk down the other side of the street. This extreme form of social punishment isn't practiced overtly in American companies, but many managers have carried it on in its verbal form. They verbally abuse their subordinates and sometimes their peers by verbal scenarios of attitudinal ostracizing—"here's how everyone else feels about you." The cruelly intended result is remarkably similar to the effect intended by physical ostracizing: the abuser wants the targeted person to feel universally disrespected, shamed, and disliked.

Example (boss to an employee): "I don't like to be the one to tell you this, but a lot of people have been coming to my office to complain about your appearance. I'm not going to name names, but the majority of the people you seem to be friendly with in the office are really upset by the clothes you are choosing, and what you're doing, or not doing, with your hair and makeup. They all spend a lot of money on themselves to present an upscale, smart professional appearance. But they say that you're bringing everyone down because you just don't look fashionable or well put together most days. I'm just telling you what I hear from everyone else."

10. *"I experience verbal abuse when my boss explodes at me, then storms out of my office to cool down."* Not all verbal abuse makes use of many words. One exasperated, "Shit, Donna!" on the boss's part, with the dramatic turning on his heel to stomp away, can be verbally abusive in the extreme. All that is not said—"I'm disappointed and frustrated at your performance on this crucial project, and here's why"—*needs* to be said so that Donna understands her mistake, or at least has a chance to clarify her intentions. But none of that helpful interaction can take place after the boss hurls his insult at Donna and then physically removes himself from any further conversation.

These are the bosses who have become used to the "blowup, then apologize" style of management. They sincerely believe that their sheepish return to Donna's office a few hours later—"I'm sorry I blew up like that. I was just having a bad day"—will erase the traumatic effects of their earlier verbal explosion. Not so.

Verbal assaults, like physical assaults, leave psychological scars on the victims that are not quickly or easily erased.

Donna, in this case, sits for hours steaming under the cloud of her boss's insult and, even after his inevitable apology, is left wondering when the next blowup will come. In miniature, what she experiences is not unlike Post Traumatic Stress Disorder (PTSD), in which victims of sudden, deeply painful and frightening violence (in her case, verbal in nature) live in a comet's tale of anxiety and apprehension. It would not be unusual for the boss's outburst to be played out in Donna's bouts with sleeplessness, inability to focus on work tasks with any enthusiasm, and recurring doubts about her competence.

Example (manager to subordinate): "I read what you wrote for my management evaluation. All I can say is go to hell!" (Walks out.)

11. *"I think I am being verbally abused by shock language my boss uses to punctuate his messages."* Cattle ranchers commonly make use of a "shock stick"—a high-voltage, battery-powered rod used to move cattle along or separate a particular animal from the herd. Although managers can't bring shock sticks to the workplace to "motivate" their employees, they nonetheless use the high voltage zingers of bullying language to underline the importance of a task, get a rise out of workers, and instill a fear factor that, at least for a short while, maximizes performance.

Like any shock, the sudden language sting of the moment must differ in intensity and quality from the other language that makes up the manager's message. Bullying language is replete with phrases that communicate disrespect ("Don't be an idiot!"), ridicule ("see if your MBA taught you anything"), threat ("don't make me take this upstairs"), and crude insult ("Fuck your excuses, just do it!"). Except for a momentary lurch, the end result of

such language used on workers isn't the forward movement the manager had intended, but instead its polar
opposite: loss of loyalty to the boss and the company,
resentment for ill treatment, and eagerness to seek work
elsewhere (preferably for a competitor!).

Example (boss to subordinate manager): "Look,
Johnson, we need to move this goddamn inventory any
way we can. Forget your ass-licking commission for a second, and just move the stuff for whatever you can get.
You act like you don't give a fuck for our bottom line
unless you get your piece of the action."

Chapter 8

Verbal Abuse, Productivity, and Health

We have all had our feelings hurt at least once in our work lives. Verbal abuse and its impact is not merely a matter of hurt feelings—"the boss spoke unkindly to me!" Instead, it is an irresponsible act that harms the target individual and the company in at least eight ways:

1. Victims of verbal abuse "go to ground" in their visibility, contributions, and effort. It is not uncommon, following an incident of verbal abuse, to see the victim literally shrunken in their desk chair, head held low. As the expression goes, we wish we could climb into a hole and let the earth swallow us up. Although these victims usually cannot afford to literally disappear from the workplace, they do disappear as valuable members of the work team.

2. Verbal abuse instantly destroys trust, not only between the verbal abuser and the victim, but also between the verbal abuser and all those who hear about the abuse and fear that they too may be targeted in the future. With the disappearance of trust comes the disappearance of risk-taking. Victims and observers of verbal abuse "play it safe" by squelching their contributions to company creativity, innovation, and experimentation.

3. If verbal abuse happens within a team, supportive working relations among impacted team members quickly crumble. Figuratively, each person on the team goes back to their solitary corner to lick their wounds and consider their options. The previous gung ho spirit of the team is replaced by dreary meetings where no one wants to speak up for fear of verbal attack.

4. Personal productivity of a victim plummets as motivation drains away and discouragement sets in. Interestingly, productivity for the verbal abuser also appears to fall off, since their time may have to be devoted to meetings

with superiors, intervention training from HR, and re-
newed team building efforts with subordinates.

5. The scene is set for payback, a push-and-pull battle
of wits that can occupy both the verbal abuser and his
victims for months or years into the future. In some exit
interviews, employees recount how "it feels good to quit.
I'm finally getting away from Manager X" (perhaps someone they worked for years ago). Department politics become byzantine games of getting back at one another for
unresolved verbal conflicts.

6. The career paths of both the perpetrator and the
victim of verbal abuse immediately plateaus and may go
into decline. Promotions and other company recognitions
may be put on hold until grievances, complaints, and ill
feelings are satisfactorily resolved.

7. The health record of those involved in the stress of
verbal abuse takes a turn for the worst. Sick days multiply
as employees try to "duck" their tormentors. Worker's
compensation claims for stress-related psychological injury at work prove increasingly common and expensive
for the company.

8. Turnover skyrockets, and with it the expense of re-
cruiting, hiring, and training replacement employees. (The
American Management Association estimates that a company will pay approximately one year's salary to replace a

midlevel manager.) If verbal abuse is tolerated within a company and becomes endemic, hiring can be made difficult by the tarnished reputation that precedes the company. No matter what the pay, the word on the street that a particular company is "a terrible place to work" can send the best candidates elsewhere.

Human relations expert Dr. Susan Elgin has her own list of the personal dangers of practicing or enduring verbal abuse.

♦   "Hostile language can kill you as surely as hostile driving can...Hostile language hurts, frustrates, and confuses people...the damage takes place over time, and the wounds aren't readily visible.

♦   Exposure to chronic verbal abuse doesn't leave you with obvious cuts and bruises, but it is a guaranteed recipe for ulcers, migraine headaches, high blood pressure, allergy attacks, accidents in the home and on the highway, colds, rashes, depression, and every sort of misery.

♦   Angry, cynical people are five times as likely to die under 50 as people who are calm and trusting (*The New York Times*, January 17, 1989).

♦   Scientists have long noted an association between social relationships and health. People who are more socially isolated, or less socially integrated, are less healthy, psychologically and physically, and more likely to die (*Science*, June 19, 1988).

♦   These effects don't show up on the short-term, which is why it took so long to find out what was really happening. In the short term, it often looks as if the meanest, angriest, least liked people are the ones getting the benefits. It took today's computers, which can find the patterns in the data from hundreds of thousands of health histories extending over lifetimes, to show us what the real facts are. They are not the facts you see on television.

◆   People who are too angry to listen cannot be educated.

◆   Research has shown that attentive listening is actually good for your health. When you are really listening, your blood pressure goes down, your heartbeat moderates, and your body shows the healthful changes associated with relaxation.

◆   When your language behavior makes other people enjoy being around you and look forward to talking with you, when you clean up your language environment so that verbal violence isn't a routine part of your life, you do more for your health and well-being than you could ever accomplish in any other way."[1]

Fear as a Response to Abusive Language

Management consultant James B. Berger points to the disrupting and corrosive influence of fear as the active agent involved in abusive language confrontations: "I believe that fear hurts productivity in the workplace more than most of us suspect. I suspect that if asked, most people would say they experienced little fear in their jobs. But there are many researchers who say that fear is a major detractor from workplace productivity"[2]

The kinds of fear that Berger has in mind are the anxieties, worries, and apprehensions that occur when:

◆   *One of our colleagues has been verbally abused.* We simultaneously feel sympathy for what he or she has experienced, but also a certain degree of apprehension over "whether we will be next." The worries, large or small, detract from our focus on work-related matters and inevitably decrease our productivity.

♦   *We ourselves have been verbally attacked.* We may feel fear not only from the incident itself, but also from its implications. Will our reputation suffer as others hear about the incident? Will we face termination farther down the road? Will the boss or other verbal abuser feel that we are now "fair game" for this kind of verbal treatment in the future?

♦   *We try to deal with our feelings in the aftermath of a verbally abusive incident.* Some of us may fear our own depth of anger, resentment, and hostility. We may worry about "losing it" and quitting our jobs on the spot, no matter how devastating that move may be to our professional and personal lives. Or we may experience fear in the form of ongoing feelings of confusion and mistrust: what did he mean by what he said to me? What should I have said in response? What should I say or do now?

In all three cases, it is not difficult to see how these quite natural but hard-to-shake fears can interrupt one's concentration on the job at hand. It becomes difficult, if not impossible, to sit down in a team meeting and interact creatively and productively with someone who has been your verbal persecutor. Even as you attempt to do your work alone, it may be hard to give your best, including meeting deadlines, for a boss or other person who has embarrassed and angered you by abusive language.

The Fear of Social Rejection

A variant of such fear, as Laura Laaman writes in the *Denver Business Journal* (March 25, 2005), is "fear of rejection." Abusive language constitutes one of the most obvious forms of rejection—the face-to-face and often public denigration of your work, your professional status, your personality, and perhaps even your character. Those kinds of attacks, for businesspeople and salespeople, says Laaman, "can be terrifying, or worse—crippling. Fear can destroy productivity, sales, market share, and spirit if left unchecked."

One common venue for these reactions comes in the awkward but often necessary "cold call"—what Laaman describes as "the 500 pound gorilla" of business life. Salespeople resist cold calls, she says, "because, on some level, they can be downright frightening." In her experience working with salespeople as a coach, "just the thought of ... being blasted by rejection can make someone physically ill." [3]

Sometimes debilitating fear can be aroused by a "face" even before derogatory words are spoken. Daniel Robin, principal with the consulting firm Daniel Robin & Associates, has identified "three faces or masks: 1. a judging face, 2. an unknown face (a faceless mask that causes uncertainty), and 3. a face that we can see, but don't dare talk about." Each of these faces, he suggests, creates the "FUD factor—Fear, Uncertainty, and Doubt," that inevitably "brings up defensiveness, making it difficult to learn or focus on solving problems." [4]

These experts and consultants join in making the common point that fear leads to distraction, which immediately impacts job performance, productivity, and even one's health. Shortly after the 9/11 tragedy, management analyst Chris Wenham wrote eloquently about the hidden influence of unexpressed worries and concerns on the part of employees:

"Any employer can tell you that a distracted worker isn't very productive. If his kid is sick, or his finances are in a mess, then that's one more thing they'll be thinking about instead of their job. Personal distraction is an insidious cloud over any company because it's exceedingly hard to identify and eliminate. So employers will go to great lengths to comfort their hires. That's why most families get their health care from the breadwinner's employer, not just because the firm wants healthy workers, but because they don't want them to worry about health. Other companies will go further, such as providing access to a company lawyer, accountant, counselor, and masseuse."[5]

An employee's fear does not arrive with the daily mail, but instead is aroused most often by the demeanor and language of a company leader. Executive coach Brian Norris tells his leader-clients that, "everyone experiences feelings of anger and fear, and everyone experiences problems.... As a leader, you do not have the luxury of diminishing your employees' self-esteem in a moment of rage. Remind your management that rage and random acts of intimidation are not in the job description. Furthermore, you do not have the luxury of wearing your negative emotions on your sleeve. When we walk through that front door, we are on stage. Our every move is being watched and ultimately emulated by our employees. Therefore, we must be consistent and predictable in how we interact with our employees, and how we deal with life's challenges."[6]

Abusive Language and Physical Health

It certainly comes as no mystery to employers that upset, frustrated employees tend to take more sick days off from work than do contented workers. But are these angry employees just faking their illnesses as payback for abusive treatment at work?

This question is answered authoritatively by The American Association of Anger Management Providers (AAAMP) in their 2005 summary of anger studies and productivity:

"Anger is not just bad for workplace productivity, but also poses a serious threat to long-term employee health. In a study of doctors who graduated from the University of North Carolina, ages 25 to 50, the most angry half of the subjects were four to five times more likely to suffer heart diseases, and seven times more likely to die of any cause than those who were less angry. A further study of UNC law students showed that of the most angry quartile of attorneys, 20 percent had died by age 50, while of the lower quartile, a mere 4 percent had died. In a study of 1800 middle-aged men in a Chicago Western Electric factory, the most angry half of the men were 1.5 times more likely to develop coronary disease, 1.5 times more likely to die of any cause, and probably more likely to develop cancer. Being angry is a stronger predictor of dying young than smoking, high blood pressure, or high cholesterol."[7]

In short, if you're stewing over abusive language aimed your direction, recognize that your anger, "payback" responses, sour expressions, and general foul mood at work are all probably hurting you much worse than any impact such behavior may have on your tormentor. For the sake of your physical and professional health, act to resolve incidents of abusive language at work.

Chapter 9

Special Issues in Dealing With Verbal Abuse

In this chapter we investigate side issues and corollaries that accompany the topic of verbal abuse. Many readers will notice here aspects of verbal abuse they have found most upsetting and least discussed.

Secondhand Verbal Abuse

When a person stands "in your face," so to speak, and verbally abuses you, there is the immediate opportunity to take a stand, draw your line in the sand, and let the person know that you will not be a target for such attacks. But when verbal abuse happens behind your back, you may find it difficult both to find out what was really said, and to confront the verbal abuser and resolve the situation.

Take this scenario, for example. Barbara has had it in for Gwen ever since Gwen was selected last month to be Employee of the Year (Barbara was a close runner up). Barbara feels that Gwen cozied up to her bosses emotionally, if not physically, to win the award. In fact, Barbara has been dying to give Gwen a piece of her mind.

But instead of doing so directly, Barbara takes two coworkers, Jim and Neil, aside: "Gwen will stab you in the back the first chance she gets. Believe me, you can't trust her. She smiles at everyone and makes you feel like her friend, but once she gets alone with the boss she really turns the knife. Jim, I heard that she called you a loser after your project fell through last month. And Neil, she never has a good word to say about you. I'm telling you, the woman is a class A bitch. I wouldn't trust her as far as I can throw her."

Barbara is verbally abusing Gwen, not only in the name-calling she uses, but in accusations that prove to be entirely false. Gwen did not call Jim a loser, nor did she say anything negative to anyone about Neil. But the question is, what can Gwen do about such secondhand, behind-her-back verbal abuse?

One option—the one we all select most often—is simply to ignore the problem. If Gwen learns by the rumor mill that Barbara is dishing dirt about her, Gwen may decide simply to "consider the source," and let the matter go. This strategy often has merit. Knowing in advance that Barbara will deny saying anything amiss, and that Jim and Neil will play dumb out of loyalty to Barbara, Gwen feels there is nothing to be gained by confronting the issue with Barbara. In fact, Gwen reasons, such confrontation may make matters worse. She figures that smoldering bad feelings that rise and fall in intensity may be preferable to open war with a coworker and her allies. Why make a mountain out of a molehill?

But leaving matters alone becomes less of an option when Gwen discovers she isn't being invited to meetings that she should attend; that her work assignments are more numerous and more difficult than those given to others in the office; and that coworkers such as Jim and Neil are giving her the cold shoulder. Gwen feels that she must act—but how?

If she takes Barbara aside for a private "chat," Gwen knows that Barbara will angrily deny "unfounded accusations"—and will probably double her behind-the-scenes efforts to sabotage Gwen. But if Gwen starts by telling Barbara the truth—"Jim came to me and told me that you were upset with me and were calling me names behind my back"—she violates Jim's trust (he had spoken to her in confidence) and risks a future bad relationship with him.

Therefore, instead of confronting Barbara individually, Gwen opts to get all three of her coworkers together ("a brief meeting," she had called it in her invitational e-mail). Once they gather in the same room, Gwen, in a controlled, nonaccusatory way, raises the issue: "I have heard that there is some friction and misunderstanding among the four of us, and I wanted to do what I could to understand the problem and see if we can put it behind us."

In this open venue, Barbara does not have the opportunity to blatantly lie about her words to Jim and Neil. At worst, all Barbara can do is deny the problem—"I don't know what you're talking about"—and thereby lower her credibility in the eyes of Jim and Neil. At best, she will use this opportunity to be as candid as Gwen: "Well, Gwen, I just think that you're being very selfish in promoting your interest and visibility without thinking about the hard work we all do. Nobody likes to work with an opportunist."

At least the issue is now out on the table for discussion (and possible resolution), rather than festering behind closed doors. Gwen can explain how surprised she was to receive the award, and she can make Barbara, Jim, and Neil feel valued and appreciated by complimenting their work. In short, Gwen has brought her verbal abusers to the table, where any animosities and misunderstandings can be resolved.

Taking a broader view, it is important to accept the fact that business life is full of sniping comments and critical judgments about one's subordinates, peers, and especially bosses. The great majority of these diatribes never get past the watercooler; they are a form of venting by which employees express their discouragement or disappointment by zinging people who aren't present to defend themselves. Saying to a coworker that your boss is "one of the most duplicitous people I have ever met" does not automatically mean that you are verbally declaring war on your boss, or that you are getting ready to quit. In most instances, you are just "blowing off steam."

Grasping that people talk about others in business, you may decide to choose battles worth fighting, rather than rising to the bait every time you hear that your name was mentioned somewhat critically outside of your hearing. A certain tolerance on your part in recognizing that "people will talk" will keep you from exhausting your energies in trying to make sure that all people, at all times, are only speaking well of you.

Reacting to What You Hear, Not What You Assume

In the stinging moments after an incident of verbal abuse, we all think of "what I should have said"—words that mysteriously left us at the moment of the abuse. Whether our response to verbal abuse happens at the moment, or during a follow-up conversation or confrontation, we must be sure we are reacting to the person's words, not to what we assume are the person's motives behind those words.

Here are five of the most common erroneous assumptions we make about someone who speaks to us in an abusive way. (Note that these assumptions may sometimes be true; the point here is that we do not know them to be true. Lacking such knowledge, we cannot base our response on what we "thought" the person meant.)

1. *"She spoke to me that way because Joan has her ear."* If you follow the "Joan" theory in framing your response to abusive language, you will end up overlaying all your bad feelings and anxieties associated with the third person onto your attempt to stop abusive language from the immediate person speaking to you. You may be right about

Joan's influence, but until you are sure of that fact, address only the abusive language before you. Don't let Joan insert words that the speaker did not in fact say.

2. *"He's still mad about my promotion."* Previous events may or may not explain why a person speaks to you abusively. By automatically assuming that the person is jealous or angry over some past event, you close off the possibility of hearing what was actually said and dealing with it in the moment. Prejudging people's motives makes everything they say—even "good morning"—subject to negative interpretation ("he's just saying that to make up for what he said last week").

3. *"She knows what I told Vickie about her."* When we experience verbal abuse, we should not assume that the person has it out for us because they found out about some wrong we had done them in the past.

A famous "Got milk?" commercial features a young couple in the middle of the night. The wife finds an empty milk carton in the refrigerator and asks her husband (who is in the other room), "Dear, is there something you forgot to tell me?" He goes on to confess a variety of secrets, including his time in prison, only to discover that she was only asking about the empty milk carton. In the same way, we can trip ourselves up by assuming or inventing problems that the speaker may not have in mind.

4. *"He spoke to me that way because he hates all women."* One of the great Houdini escapes from dealing with personal attacks is to hide ourselves in the mantle of

our larger class. If we are men, we rationalize that the speaker's abusive language can be explained because she "has a problem with men." If we are women, we silently accuse the speaker of being a misogynist.

Although these explanations sometimes prove true, we always need to confront and deal with the strong possibility that the speaker is addressing abusive language to us as individuals, not to our class. The question then becomes "Why is she treating *me* this way and what can I do about it?" This is a far more appropriate response than asking, "Why is she treating men (or women) this way, and what can they do about it?"

5. *"She yelled at me just to get me to yell back at her. Then she could fire me."* It's dangerous to decide in advance that a verbal abuser has a particular strategy in mind. Emotional outbursts often do not arise from carefully calculated plans. In any case, what a verbal abuser says to you does not force you to do anything ("she made me call her names"). Leave yourself free to choose the best among your options by not attributing an entire game plan to someone who may be running only one play.

Verbal Abuse at the Edges

We should not make the mistake of thinking that verbal abusers are always "out of control," and unconscious of the risk they run by violating company management policies, general work rules, and pillars of company culture. Verbal abusers, in fact, can cleverly weave their message so that it gets its harsh message to the targeted people intended, while leaving the verbal abuser free to say, "I was speaking in general, not to specific people." In this way, company leaders are often able to deliver searing rages filled with foul words, but escape, through a technicality, the charge of verbally abusing individual employees.

Here's an example. Paula has joined a group of fellow employees for the weekly meeting of the New Products Promotion task force.

The boss, who has just seen some negative numbers for the quarter, comes in screaming, "Stupidity and laziness are not going to cut it around here anymore." He continues this tirade upon his surprised employees: "I'm tired of walking through the office and seeing idiots surfing the Internet while pretending to work. All I can say is that the bastards who aren't doing their jobs right now had better not come crying to me when the next round of layoffs occurs. Goddamn it, all I'm asking for is some commitment to innovation, creativity, and new ideas to help get our latest products off to a good start."

The boss stomps out of the room, leaving Paula and her coworkers stunned and shaken. The boss felt he could avoid the implications of verbally abusing or accusing any one employee by lambasting an entire group. If anyone complained about his tirade and insults to company officers, he could claim that he was angry about the situation, not angry with particular people. If workers came directly to him to discuss his blast, he could say, "If the shoe fits, wear it."

Group Action Against Verbal Abuse of the Group

The type of one-size fits all verbal abuse mentioned in the previous example should be challenged by members of the group to whom it was addressed. Here are three techniques that groups can use to cancel the free ticket of any boss who feels he or she can verbally abuse people in a broad manner without consequences:

1. *Appoint spokespeople and stand behind them.* A team of two or three representatives of the group can request to meet with the boss to register their strong opposition, on behalf of the entire group, to the tirade. This kind of civilized, orderly response has more influence on verbal abusers than any one employee complaining alone.

2. *Take the initiative and invite the verbal abuser to a problem-solving focus group, perhaps with mediation from an HR representative.* In this safe zone, members of the group can say how they felt when the verbal abuse took place. The verbal abuser can consider this an intervention of sorts, and may end up apologizing for the inappropriate diatribe.

3. *Draft a letter or e-mail to the verbal abuser, signed by all members of the group.* The danger of this kind of communication is that it has only one chance to say its

message clearly and persuasively. In addition, no group members will be present, when the message is received, to interpret what the words were intended to mean. But written carefully and without exaggeration, a letter of protest can be used to keep tempers from flaring on both sides (as they might in a face-to-face meeting). Also, a written message stands as a record in case the problem persists.

The Dangers of Blurring the Line Between Work Behavior and Nonwork Behavior

In addition to their thoughts, people also bring their feelings to work. As employees get to know one another, conversation topics become more various, more personal, and more diffuse. We have probably all experienced or overheard workplace conversations about kids, sports, vacation plans, movies, restaurants, diets, exercise routines, and countless other nonwork subjects.

But as "the way we talk at home" becomes quite similar to "the way we talk at work," the line can become blurred between what's permissible outside work and what's permitted in the workplace.

Take sudden disappointments, for example. A person who walks out to their car to see a flat tire can mutter, "Fuck!" without fear of being arrested. (We're not condoning this language, but simply pointing out that in private life we each have the freedom to use it.) A manager who draws no clear line between such nonwork expressions of feeling and what's appropriate at work could easily find oneself in a meeting looking at poor third quarter numbers and moaning out loud, "Aw, fuck!" While that sentiment might precisely capture their own feeling at the time, it is also sure to offend some members of the group.

Taking this real possibility of a language slip to its logical extension, managers and others who use yelling, swearing, and implied threats as a regular part of their nonwork life are prone to carrying these language forms into the workplace (especially if these people have had a modicum of success from its usage—that is, if the kids really do jump to clean their rooms when dad bellows, "Get your asses upstairs and clean those rooms!"). When it comes time to motivate employees to get something done, it's tempting for managers to fall back on the language they used successfully in nonwork situations.

One narrative makes this problem quite clear. Nathan T. manages a shipping center for a well-known package express service. Until last year, he held a similar position as a sergeant in the military.

"I don't have to tell you that the language in that environment was pretty crude." Nathan said, describing his previous experience. "We hardly ever spoke about a truck driver without attaching some string of swear words to describe the lazy mother. When something went wrong, we had a regular ritual of swearing up a storm to mark the occasion, indicate our feelings about it, and vent some of our frustration."

However, Nathan found he experienced a culture shock of sorts when he entered the civilian workplace. "Once I got out of the service and got this job on the outside, it was difficult for me to watch my mouth," he said. "I noticed that no one else in the organization felt free to swear about people or situations. When one truck driver heard me call him a 'stupid SOB,' he reported it immediately to his union representative and I had to sit through some sensitivity training sessions for a week. I've learned at this point that language has consequences. Even though I'm thinking some pretty foul things about the screwups that happen during the workday, I try not to express them in four-letter words. But it's damn hard at times."

Verbal Abuse as a Means of Curtailing Dialogue

Many instances of verbal abuse occur not at the beginning of a conversation ("Good morning, Susan. By the way, I think you're a whining slut."), but rather during the middle of a conversation that has grown uncomfortable for the verbal abuser.

For example, consider this dialogue between an IT manager, Cal, and one of his equipment installers, Phillip.

CAL: I thought I told you to run #16 cable to all the South Wing offices.

PHILLIP: You might have meant #16, but you told me #18, so that's what I ran. I wondered at the time if you had made a mistake.

CAL (getting heated): You wondered but you didn't ask me? What would it take, ten seconds just to check if you're doing the right thing on a four-day job?

PHILLIP: Look, you sounded certain about the #18 wire, so I didn't challenge you. I think I even got an e-mail.

CAL (getting abusive): That's a bunch of crap, Phillip. I told you to run #16 cable and you ran #18 instead. You didn't check with me because you knew you had fucked up big time.

PHILLIP (stunned, not knowing what to say): Look, I really thought you wanted #18.

CAL (continuing to rage): But now you're not sure, right? All you cared about was covering your ass, so you made up a good story. This is your last chance, buddy. Another screw up like this and your ass is on the line.

Midway through this conversation, Cal senses that Phillip may indeed be right, and that it was his own fault was for this expensive wiring mistake. Cal uses abusive language (signaled by his first use of foul language) to shut Phillip down. Cal doesn't want Phillip to explain about the e-mail he received specifying the #18 cable, so Cal raises the intensity of his rant to such a level that Phillip backs off, for fear of provoking Cal even further.

When you sense that verbal abuse is being used against you as a silencing technique, make an effort to press on long enough to get your key claims and evidence on the table. Once a verbal abuser recognizes that you "have the goods" on them, they tend to take a new tact and abandon the bluster of verbal rage. That new tact, of course, may also involve verbal abuse under a different guise (lies, for example) that contradicts your memory of the abusive situation.

In the following diagram, we see how verbal abuse can be used to harden the "shell," or entry points, surrounding the context of a message. For anyone to understand the full message, they must first pass through the context of that message (what were the circumstances? what was the intended audience? what was our attitude toward the message?) to reach its content or "dictionary meaning." Those who want to prevent messages from being understood or discussed (let's say, a controversial idea that comes up in a meeting) may launch into verbal abuse directed against one or more members of the group. This strategy forms a hard layer around the context of the message and prevents further efforts at understanding. Under the barrage of verbal abuse, group members may whisper to one another, "Don't go there. He obviously isn't ready to discuss it."

Verbal abuse acts to harden the shell around context by promising negative consequences to anyone who dares to probe that context on the way to content. In effect, the verbal abuser demonstrates to an individual, and by extension to anyone who hears about their treatment of the individual, that efforts to move beyond the shell into context and content will be greeted by punishing verbal assaults.

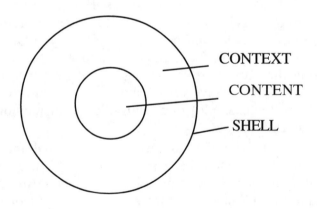

Verbal Abuse as Warning Signs of Hostile Intent

Most mammals display obvious signals that they are ready to do battle. Horses put their ears back and stick out their teeth. Dogs growl, curl back their lips and prickle up the hair along their spines. Some fish turn colors when annoyed, or expand to twice their ordinary size. Peacocks and turkeys spread their tail feathers to make themselves look larger and fiercer.

Except for the color that may redden in our cheeks as blood pressure rises, we human beings don't have bodily ways of signaling that we are getting hostile. We have invented some nonverbal signals, of course, such as "flipping the bird" or raising a fist. But our primary signal that our temperature is figuratively reaching the boiling point lies in our use of strong language. As if placing warning signs on a road, we signal to others not to "go farther down this road unless you want to crash." If more than one such sign is necessary, we make the signs larger, more dramatic, and more emphatic in the both the words we choose and the volume and tone that accompanies them.

In the following dialogue, notice how Ruth, a midlevel manager, uses increasingly abusive language to derail her subordinate's (Ralph's) explanation of why he can't attend a scheduled business trip. Ruth does not want Ralph to go down the road of that subject, so she sets up a series of increasingly obvious and abusive language signs to shut him up and shut him down.

RALPH: I've got some bad news about that business trip you wanted me to take next week.

RUTH (first sign of hostility): I don't want to hear it, Ralph. It's your turn to travel.

RALPH: But hear me out. My first reason—

RUTH (with rising hostility): Damn it, Ralph, are you deaf? You're going on that business trip. Period.

RALPH: But I can't. My mother is—

RUTH (now abusive): Your mother, your sister, your father, your goldfish. I've heard every excuse from you I'm going to take. It's your turn to travel and you're not going to get out of it. God, I'm amazed you'd even ask.

RALPH: I just wanted to—

RUTH (giving her final abusive signal): Stop, Ralph. You are going on the fucking trip. That's it.

RALPH (giving in): Okay, okay. There's no need to get hostile. I'll work it out somehow.

As a mental traveler down this road, be aware when someone begins using verbal abuse to put up stop signs in order prevent you from reaching your destination. A useful technique at the first occurrence of such signs is to create a detour that takes you to you goal without provoking further verbal abuse.

Here's a redo of Ralph's conversation with Ruth. This time Ralph makes use of a clever detour technique.

RALPH: I've got some bad news about that business trip you wanted me to take next week.

RUTH (first sign of hostility): I don't want to hear it, Ralph. It's your turn to travel.

RALPH (sensing hostility and inventing a detour): Fine, let's not talk about the trip. How is your mother doing?

RUTH: About the same. She likes her present convalescent hospital better than the old one.

RALPH: I'm facing the same kind of situation. My mother just can't care for herself alone anymore. She fell twice last week, and there was no one there to help her.

RUTH: That's awful. Can you get her into a place near her home?

RALPH: There's one opening, but I have to act quickly before someone else takes it.

RUTH: Take a day off to do this if you have to. It's important.

RALPH: You could really help me out if I could postpone the business trip by just a few days. That way I could get her all moved in before something serious happens.

RUTH: No problem. In fact, let me ask around to see if anyone else will take that trip. I know it's your turn, but under the circumstances I'm sure someone will pinch hit for you.

In this case, Ralph does not continue blithely driving down the road Ruth doesn't want him to take. Instead, he reaches his goal by a different route, in this case getting Ruth to identify emotionally with the dilemma he faces with his elderly mother. Verbal abuse can often be eliminated simply by creativity (a preferable word to trickery) on the part of the potential victim.

The Fine Line Between Verbal Abuse and Physical Violence

Although your office may be an exception to the rule, thousands of incidents of physical violence (most of them unreported to law agencies) occur in American corporations every year. These can range from a pushing match to a punch on the nose, or from a slap across the face to a full-out brawl (the latter preferred by legislative bodies in some countries). The worst case scenario of physical violence is the crazed employee who brings in a gun, a bomb, or poison to kill his coworkers.

What spawns such terrible and desperate acts of frustration and anger? In most explosions of physical violence, prior verbal abuse has lit the fuse. Consider the following case among too many.

At California State University, Fullerton in the late 1970s, a couple employees in the Audiovisual departmental regularly teased a janitor by suggesting they possessed pornographic pictures of his wife. These cruel workers went to great length to make it seem that they had reel upon reel of film and video footage of the woman "in action." Upset to the point of distraction, the janitor went home one afternoon, loaded several guns, and came back to the AV department at the University, where he killed eight people and wounded several more.

This tragedy is symbolic of the direct connection between verbal abuse and resulting physical violence. Stop the verbal abuse and you have taken a major step toward curtailing physical violence in the workplace.

Verbal Abuse and the Grapevine

Every human organization is likely to have both an overt system of communication (meetings, speeches, briefings, and so forth), as well as a covert system of communication, commonly known as "the grapevine." This somewhat mysterious communication web does not necessarily embrace all people within an organization. Managers and supervisors, for example, often find it hard to learn "what people are saying" on the grapevine because these authority figures aren't trusted enough for full inclusion. CEOs have an even more difficult time breaking through to what rank and file employees are saying to one another about work life and the company. Sam Walton, founding CEO of Wal-Mart, resorted to Friday afternoon tailgate picnics in the parking lot of his company's headquarters in an effort to talk eye-to-eye with employees about what concerned them most.

As we will see, verbal abusers pay attention to where you are in the structure of the grapevine, and for that reason you should make an effort right now to evaluate your approximate position in this ever-changing, but always important, communication network. The following chart shows typical relationships in a company grapevine. You should take particular note of the Liaison Individuals, who can be counted on to "spread the word" to many others in the grapevine. Also note Isolates, those individuals who are dead ends for purposes of information flow. Few people share news with them, and they share news with few people. We shouldn't assume that Isolates are necessarily oddballs. Many organizations have "sole contributors" who tend to work alone and report back their results from time to time. Simply due to the nature of their work, they interface with few other employees during the day, and have few occasions to hear or share the company gossip (and perhaps less interest in doing so).

How the Grapevine Works

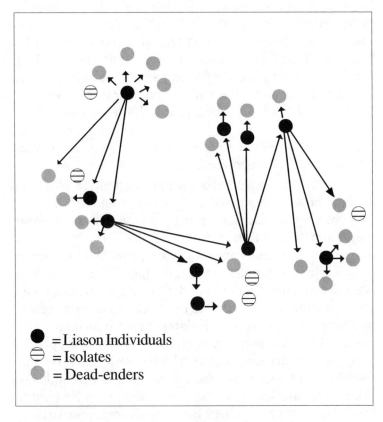

● = Liason Individuals
⊖ = Isolates
○ = Dead-enders

Verbal abusers are notorious for seeking out individuals who are relatively unprotected by the grapevine. In other words, verbal abusers turn their fury most easily toward those who can do the least damage in terms of spreading news about the abuse. For this reason, Isolates certainly come in for more than their share of verbal attacks and assaults. They have few if any confidants in the grapevine with whom to share the details of the abuse incident.

By contrast, Liaison Individuals experience less verbal abuse. They are capable within minutes of letting several people within the organization know that they are under attack. And within a day or two, hundreds of people may have heard the news ("Did you hear what Linda's boss said to her? Can you believe it?").

Grapevine messages were traditionally spread by word of mouth at locations such as coffee rooms and hallway watercoolers. In addition to those physical sites, we now make heavy use of electronic communication devices such as e-mail and, to a lesser extent, voicemail. Because some companies see the grapevine as a potentially subversive, dangerous force, they have tried to curtail "personal use" of e-mail and voicemail by letting their employees know that these channels are monitored (that is, listened in on) by management. The result, of course, is a chilling effect on the willingness of employees to spread "hot news" and rumors by electronic means.

But the grapevine is resilient in its ability to find ways for its member individuals to make contact. Like a blood circulation system blocked at one artery, the grapevine grows detour capillaries so that communication can continue. Employees who can't share inside information and unapproved comments with one another at work quickly get one another's home e-mail addresses and carry on communication in that way. If coffee rooms and watercoolers turn out to be dangerous places for grapevine information, employees will quickly opt for after work get-togethers at nearby restaurants and watering holes.

The grapevine proves particularly effective when verbal abuse comes from a company leader. He or she is not usually eager to sacrifice status in the company (and subsequent progress on his or her career path) for the momentary satisfaction, such as it is, of verbally abusing a target employee. Getting connected and staying involved with the grapevine is a wise countermeasure and an excellent prophylactic against the possibility of being singled out for verbal attack.

Chances are you have already joined your company's grapevine without even knowing it. Think for a moment about your business day and ordinary contacts with others. From whom do you typically hear rumors about plans, changes, personalities, and problems in the company? Once you hear such information, with whom do you typically share it? These relationships are your primary ties to the grapevine.

If you wish, you can increase your grapevine involvement by seeking out more people with whom to disclose information. These new contacts come at a risk, of course, because you do not know in advance how people will deal with the information or feelings you share with them. New lines of connection tend to follow old lines of trust in the grapevine: you share with those you have come to know well and to trust.

Verbal Abuse and the Tattletale Problem

In public schools, the most extreme forms of physical abuse upon students are highly visible and generally receive swift attention and action. When a teacher "loses it" and slaps a student across the face, the prima facie case is immediately compelling and sends a whole battery of administrative review measures into action. But the great majority of incidents of physical abuse do not present themselves so clearly.

What happens in the case of the "middle ground" abuses? Consider the following examples: a teacher firmly grips a student's shoulder and leaves finger marks; a teacher shoves a book across the desk at a student, bumping their chest; a teacher violently shakes the desk of a student who has dozed off. Victims are slower to report these types of incidents, and administrators are slower to act when they are reported. The case is even more ambiguous when a fellow student has struck out against another student in some way. "Do I tell or not?" is the question often asked.

The situation is not dissimilar from verbal abuse in American companies. The most extreme cases (a boss cursing out an employee in front of others, in the foulest of language) are quickly reported, easily documented, and generally dealt with swiftly. Less obvious offenses, however, raise the tattletale question for victims of verbal abuse. Should I really go to my boss's boss over this incident? Will I seem like a wimp who can't fight my own battles? Will bosses all hang together no matter what? Was it really that bad, or am I exaggerating things just because I'm mad and my feelings were hurt?

The option of going above your boss (whether to HR, your boss's boss, or some other authority or mediator) is often unavailable in some companies, and many times not an option at all in military organizations. The unspoken imperative in such environments is not to break ranks or "talk out of school." To break this rule poses the substantial risk of career suicide. In other words, your boss's boss may agree to hear you out, but you will never be able to go back to your old work unit again without a dark cloud over your head in the form of bad work assignments, poor performance evaluations, and strained working relationships. In these circumstances, you may wisely decide to fight your battles locally within your work group, rather than attempting to appeal your case to some higher authority. (Obviously this general advice does not

apply to overt and actionable abuse such as sexual harassment which violates not only workplace propriety but
state and federal law. Those kinds of incidents should,
and must be reported, no matter what the formal or informal hierarchy rules are within the organization.)

Some companies, fortunately, have seen the advantage
of opening various channels for the expression and filing
of complaints and grievances. Some corporate vice presidents, for example, have regular "open door" hours when
any employee in their division can come to discuss any
matter. Ombudsmen and HR counselors serve a similar
function—somewhere to go and someone to tell if you have
experienced verbal abuse. Still, victims naturally worry
about what will happen once they open the Pandora's box
of "going public" (at least within the company) about the
abuse they suffered.

In deciding whether and how to report an incident of
verbal abuse, you will want to find answers to at least four
questions:

1. *Will my confidentiality be respected?* Recognize in
this regard that the verbal abuser you have accused will
have to be made aware of the charges against them. In
most cases, he will surmise who reported him, even if the
company has assured you that "your name will not be used."

2. *Am I asking for action or for advice?* Companies may
be quite successful in offering you a cloak of anonymity
while you discuss the incident of verbal abuse with a counselor and receive advice on what to do. As mentioned above,
that anonymity may vanish if you are asking the company
to take disciplinary action against the verbal abuser.

3. *What is my goal?* Decide in advance whether you want to leave your present work situation, perhaps by means of a transfer. You may instead prefer that a mediator help you resolve the incident of verbal abuse by bringing all parties together. You may also want to press your rights within the company, and perhaps within the law, to see that the verbal abuser is punished. If you know in advance what you are trying to achieve, your chances of success are greatly improved.

4. *What are the risks of trying to resolve the situation by myself?* Can you approach the verbal abuser to express your feelings and receive an apology? Or will further contact lead to further verbal abuse? Are you too angry to meet with the verbal abuser, or they with you? Is there a risk that the abuser will dominate conversation in such a way that you won't get to express your perspective? Will your action open you up to work-related threats from the abuser?

None of these issues is raised with the thought of talking you out of reporting verbal abuse. Nevertheless, it would be naïve to give the impression that all, or even most, companies contain the appropriate channels, confidentiality provisions, and "retribution insurance" to ensure your professional well-being during and after the reporting process. Get to know how your report will be handled within your organization to make sure that your interests, already attacked by verbal abuse, are not further threatened.

Chapter 10

A Toolbox of
20 Techniques to
Stop Verbal Abuse

Summarized here are nearly two dozen techniques for avoiding, interrupting, challenging, and ultimately stopping, incidents of verbal abuse. (Please note that the companion strategies developed for verbal abusers themselves—how to quit abusing—are found in the *Ten Commandments for Managers* section in chapter five.) You must be the judge of which of these techniques fits your personality, purpose, and circumstance best. A wide variety of tools are provided so that if one doesn't work, you can try others. Paraphrasing the song title, here you have 20 ways to leave your bother. Each technique is phrased in the words of a warrior facing up against verbal abuse in the workplace.

Technique one: "I catch my boss at the first sign that the conversation is going to turn nasty and abusive. I hold up my hand and insist that he 'Wait!' I calmly explain that I'm not going to be a target for verbal abuse. If he can speak to me in a decent manner, I will be glad to talk. Otherwise I'm going back to my desk until he cools down."

Technique two: "I grab the first abusive phrase and force my boss to repeat what he just said. For example, if he says, 'You Mexicans are all alike in this company,' I won't let it pass. 'Say that again,' I tell him. 'I want to make sure I heard what you said.' If he does have the foolishness to repeat his racist or sexist remark, I point out to him that he is violating Title VII and EEOC [Equal Employment Opportunity Commission] laws, and that he could lose his job for making racist or sexist remarks to me. Usually he doesn't repeat the bad sentence. He catches himself, realizes what he has said, and either apologizes or proceeds in a more respectful tone."

Technique three: "If I know I'm walking into a confrontation with a verbal abuser, I will take a friend along as an observer. If my boss says, 'I want to talk to you alone,' I say that my coworker will stay as a witness to the fact that the conversation wasn't verbally abusive. If he continues to insist that my friend leave, I press my point that I need verification of what took place in the conversation in case my rights are violated and I need to take further action. This usually shuts him up. He will either continue the conversation without verbal abuse, with my friend standing there, or will guarantee me that no verbal abuse will take place, in which case I ask my friend to wait outside the door."

Technique four: "Before putting myself in harm's way by engaging in a conversation with a verbal abuser, I go to HR and, without mentioning names, tell them that I need some advice on how to cope with someone who violates the company code of conduct with their verbally abusive habits. In the two times I've done this, HR has always insisted that the conversation between me and the potential verbal abuser take place in their office. They are not in the room, but simply changing the location to one of their offices puts the abuser on notice that he had better not mouth off."

Technique five: "When I face a conversation that I know will be heated and may turn verbally abusive, I take charge of the conversation right from the beginning, even if the other person has called me into their office. I start out with something like, 'I assume you want to talk about the misunderstanding about Eileen's vacation time, and I know we both have very strong feelings about this. What I would like to do is listen to your point of view without responding for a few minutes, and then I would like you to give me the same courtesy to tell my perspective. How does that sound

to you?' There are no guarantees, of course, but my use of
the word 'courtesy' and my willingness to listen to them
first, usually produces a conversation that may be strongly
worded, but not verbally abusive."

Technique six: "When someone simply lights into me
in a verbally abusive way, before I have a chance to respond at all, I 'vote with my feet' and step away from the
situation. I reason that they can't have a conversation if
there aren't two people there to converse. When I get four
or five steps away, I turn and say in as calm a voice as I
can muster, 'I do want to talk with you about these issues.
But I won't be yelled at or insulted. Let me know when
you would like to continue.' Then I walk away. If the person is really out of control and follows me to my office,
screaming at me all the while, I will either dial security or
walk to some secure place (I've used the women's room
once) to avoid the verbal abuse. I don't feel that I am
hiding out. I am simply removing myself from the situation until it calms down. And it usually does within a few
minutes."

Technique seven: "When I'm caught in a public situation, such as a meeting or a briefing with many other people
in the room, I know I can't depend on anyone else to speak
up in my defense once verbal abuse starts. They are all too
afraid that the boss will turn his fury on them. So I practice what I call 'Face the Bully' and it usually works. Once
someone starts getting personal and insulting, I simply
stand up and take a couple steps toward them. I don't say
anything, but just let them rant on until they have to take
a breath (most verbal abusers are shouting loud enough

that they have to breathe often). When that breath comes, I use a calm, forceful voice to say, 'Are you finished?' and stare at them. They may say, "No, I'm certainly not!" and launch into more of his rage. If this happens, I walk out and leave them bellowing to a blank spot. I won't willingly be the target of verbal abuse. But if they do stop, which is quite likely, I say, 'You are verbally abusing me, which is against the policies of this company and against the law. Do you want to continue this conversation in a more civilized manner?' That warning tends to call them up short and changes the tone of the confrontation. At best, they will apologize and start over in a more respectful tone."

Technique eight; "If a conversation with my boss turns abusive, I catch him on each and every word that I find offensive. Loud enough for him to hear above his own voice, I say little phrases like "that word offends me," "that word is verbal abuse," "that word is illegal in the workplace," and "that word violates company policies." Peppering him with these quick objections has the result of throwing him off track from what he wanted to say and getting him to trim out the language that I'm complaining about. It also lets him know that I'm not going to sit there with my head hung low, listening to his rant."

Technique nine: "I can usually spot a verbally abusive incident coming up, especially when the person has a reputation in the office for being an abuser. An hour or so before I'm scheduled to go into the lion's den, I e-mail or drop off a short paragraph that says something along these lines: 'I look forward to speaking with you at 2 p.m. Because the topic is difficult for both of us to talk about without anger, I'm attaching a page from the Company Handbook that describes harassment and abuse, including verbal abuse. I'm confident that you will take these words to heart before we speak.' By putting him on notice in this way, I usually walk into a calmer conversation."

Technique 10: "The verbal abuse I'm subjected to takes the form of nasty little jabs said to me in passing, rather than in a face-to-face meeting. My boss comments on my hair, my clothing, my perfume, my shoes, my makeup, my purse—anything she knows will make me irritated. Obviously I can't hide all these things from her view, nor do I want to. And I know that she will keep this up as long as she knows it peeves me. So I keep a journal—a big, visible one—open on my desk. The second she begins with one of her carping, insulting statements, I say, 'Could you speak a little slower? HR said that I should write down exactly what you said in my journal.' That has an amazing effect in shutting her down. She still gives me disapproving stares, but at least the verbal abuse has stopped completely."

Technique 11: "I use questions to make the verbal abuser realize what he is doing and saying. At the first occurrence of a verbally offensive statement, I interrupt to say, 'Do you really want to continue in this way?' or 'Are you thinking carefully about what you are saying right now?' or 'Do you want a chance to rephrase what you just said to me?' or 'How would you feel if your boss knew you were speaking to me in this way?' I don't scream out these questions, because I know that my calm manner keeps me in the driver's seat. I figure that he can't keep up his diatribe if I keep up my steady questions."

Technique 12: "I use the 'time out' technique to give the verbal abuser time to calm down. I'm a big believer in giving people a moment to think about what they are doing, and to let their emotions settle. So when a conversation starts getting too heated or personally insulting for me, I say, 'Time out! Let's both take a minute just to sit here and then continue.' If I say this forcefully enough, he will comply. We sit there staring at the wall or at the floor. But when conversation continues, it is on a much more even keel."

Technique 13: "I went to HR and asked them to either develop their own in-house seminar on verbal abuse, or bring someone in from the outside for a seminar. Then I made all the people I supervise go through the training session. To put teeth in the issue, I made 'respectful interaction with colleagues' one of the categories in their performance evaluation, which I have to fill out twice a year. The big bosses in this company aren't good at avoiding verbal abuse, but I reason that we can 'trickle up' the right way of relating by educating the rank-and-file employees first."

Technique 14: "After two incidents of verbal abuse from midlevel managers in the company, I asked one of the senior vice presidents to take a moment in her next speech to us for a no-nonsense sermon on what she expected and would not tolerate in terms of verbal interaction between employees. Having a high level person 'lay down the law' to all of us, including the two most notorious abusers, has stopped verbal abuse in its tracks around here."

Technique 15: "It's a simple trick, but it has always worked for me. When I walk into a situation that I know is emotionally charged, I carry a mini tape recorder. At the first occurrence of a personal attack or foul language, I interrupt and say, 'Excuse me, I just wanted everyone to know that I'm taping this meeting, which is my right according to the Director of HR.' Of course the verbal abusers involved never let me go on taping. They say something like, 'Okay, okay, we get the point. Turn off that blasted thing and we'll watch what we say.' I agree with their request, but let them know that it's going back on if they don't keep their word."

Technique 16: "I learned this trick from a deaf friend of mine. When someone starts blasting verbal abuse into my face, I hold up both hands, palms out, and look them in the eye. The gesture is so unusual that it stops them dead. When they pause to figure out what I'm doing, I calmly say, 'This is verbal abuse. It's bad for me, and it's also bad for you in terms of the legal trouble you'll bring on yourself. Do you want to start over?' Almost always the person sheepishly says, 'Okay, let's start over.'"

Technique 17: "This technique isn't particularly courageous, but it works like a charm. If I'm going in to a meeting with my boss and I know he's really steamed about something, I just take in two cups of coffee. Before he launches into his carefully planned verbal assault, I throw him off by kindly offering him a cup of coffee. If he starts in anyway with his verbal abuse, I interrupt to say, 'Do you want some sugar?' This technique has worked so well for me that I've never had to get to the 'Do you want some cream?' line."

Technique 18: "In really offensive cases of verbal abuse, I don't try to play games or save face for the abuser. I just draw my line in the sand. I say clearly, 'You are verbally abusing me. I'm going to stop this conversation right now and report this incident to HR and other appropriate officers in this company. If necessary, I will use legal means to keep you from talking to me or anyone else in this way.' Then I walk away. Almost inevitably, I get a knock at my office door about 15 minutes later with an apology. No manager wants to be the subject of a harassment and abuse investigation."

Technique 19: "Some verbal abusers are actually pretty decent people who just lose control of their tongues from time to time, maybe because they talk that way at home. If I like the person and want to help them change, I use the phrase, 'You can't say that' every time they make a foul remark, tell an offensive joke, make a racial slur, or some other stupid slipup. I don't say my phrase judgmentally—it's just a flat out declaration. The person stops and asks, 'Why not? That's when I have them. I launch into my own sermon about HR policies, workplace dignity and decency, and the court cases that have awarded hundreds of thousands of dollars to abused, harassed workers. I feel a bit like a missionary for decent speech in the workplace. But what's the alternative?"

Technique 20: "I use the technique popularized a number of years ago by psychologist Pete Smith. It works like this: when someone stands in your face and makes an offensive, verbally abusive accusation, you just eliminate the offensive words and say back in an accepting tone exactly what you heard. Here's an example:

ABUSER: 'You and your dyke friends don't contribute a damn thing around here!'
MY REPLY: 'You're right, my friends and I could contribute more than we do.'
ABUSER: 'And none of you bitches are getting promoted unless you shape up.'
MY REPLY: 'You're right; we will all have to work hard to get promoted.'

This is what I call mental judo—using the force of the other person to flip them over. Within a few seconds they literally don't know what to say. It has cost me nothing to agree, minus the insulting words, with the general ideas. Who among us couldn't contribute more, improve their work habits, and so forth. Verbal abusers have a game plan in mind: they attack, expecting you to counterattack or to fight fire with fire. I refuse. I would rather just flip them on their back, so to speak, by agreeing with them. It shuts them up faster than anything I know."

Epilogue

Picturing a Workplace Free From Verbal Abuse

Imagine the possibilities for a moment. You discover an unexpected but disastrous glitch in a product almost ready for release by the company. You go straight to your boss with this unfortunate but necessary information, knowing fully that he will keep his cool and not "kill the messenger."

Next, you attend a team meeting made up of representatives from each of the company's five divisions. Each individual on the team has a different set of priorities and needs, but you know from the outset of the meeting that conversation will be polite, direct, and constructive. Disagreement on issues in the company does not mean that people try to verbally tear one another apart.

The president of the company assembles the entire workforce to hear her state of the company speech in the late afternoon. She is obviously upset by sagging profits. But she expresses her disappointment directly, maturely, and powerfully without calling anyone or any division by derogatory names.

At this kind of company, employees are not afraid to take imaginative leaps and innovative risks. They know that if they fail, they will not face verbal crucifixion from their bosses. Instead, evaluation will focus on what went right and what went wrong, not who is "good" or "bad" as a person or employee. At this company, workers keep their jobs years longer than is typical for their industry. They are reasonably happy throughout the workday because they are treated with respect by their bosses and by one another. They go home feeling good about themselves as professionals. Although going to work is never as attractive as staying home, they rise each morning without much moaning to go back to a workplace they enjoy.

New drapes, fancier desks, or expensive art on the company walls do not create the secure, contented work environment we have just described. Only strict limits on interpersonal aggression, particularly in the form of verbal abuse, can achieve the "extreme makeover" of an anger-ridden, brutal workplace into a place for relationships built on trust, and astounding productivity based on freedom from fear.

Chapter Notes

Chapter 2

1. *Hardball for Women: Winning at the Game of Business.* Pat Heim, et al., Plume, 1993.

Chapter 3

1. *The Human Side of Enterprise*. Douglas Macgregor, McGraw-Hill, 1985.
2. *National Directory of Legal Employers, NALP 2000, and 2000 Catalyst Census of Women Corporate Officers and Top Earners*; 2002 Catalyst; American Medical Association.
3. "Wonder Women: Profiles of Leading Female CEOs and Business Executives." John Gettings and David Johnson.
   http://www.infoplease.com/spotwomenceo1.html.

Chapter 4

1. Cited by RP Consultants, March, 2000 (http://www.rpconsult.com) from a *Working Woman Magazine* survey.

2. Quoted from *http://www.timslaw.com/hostile-environment.htm.*

3. Cited from an actual inquiry with an online lawyer, Nov. 11, 2004 at *http://forum.freeadvice.com.*

4. Source: FindLaw for Legal Professionals (*http:library.lp.findlaw.com*), "How Much Is Enough? Difficulties Defining 'Hostile Work Environment' in Title VII Harassment Claims," by Alexis L. Pheiffer.

5. Ibid.

6. Cited in "Workplace Rudeness Is On the Rise: Vulgar Language Is Part of the Problem," in Employee Assistance: Behavioral Healthcare Solutions in Today's Managed Care Environment, accessed Dec. 8, 2004 at *http://www.cusscontrol.com/newsarticles/newpopup05.html.*

7. Ibid.

8. "On-the-Job Cursing: Obscene Talk Is the Latest Target of Workplace Ban," *The Wall Street Journal*, May 8, 2001, p. 13.

9. Ibid.

10. Eugene Volokh, "The Definition of 'Hostile Work Environment' Harassment," accessed Jan. 25, 2005 at *http://www1.law.ucla/edu.*

11. Ibid.

12. Dean J. Schaner and Melissa M. Erlemeier, "When Faith and Work Collide: Defining Standards for Religious Harassment in the Workplace," Employee Relations Law Journal, June 1, 1995, p. 26.

13. BlueCross BlueShield of Illinois, Heath Care Service Corporation's Code of Conduct: Integrity Standard, accessed Jan. 25, 2005 at *http://www.bcbsil.com/code.*

14. Sexual Harassment: Hostile Work Environment, UC-Davis Health System, accessed Jan. 25, 2005, *http://www.ucdmc.ucdavis.edu/cne/resources/report/hostile.htm*

15. New Jersey State Policy Prohibiting Discrimination, Harassment, or Hostile Environments in the Workplace, issued December 16, 1999; revised: January 7, 2002.

16. "Hostile Workplace/Hostile Work Environment—What Is It?," in *Hostile Workplace Prevention*, April 1997, accessed at *http:///www.itstime.com/apr97.htm*

Chapter 6

1. *Winning with Difficult People*, 3e, by Arthur H. Bell and Dayle M. Smith (Barron's, 2004).

Chapter 8

1. Cited in *Hostile Workplace Prevention* [on-line newsletter], April, 1997, no page.
   www.itstime.com/apr97.htm.

2. James B. Berger, "Fear in the Workplace: What Is the Real Price?," accessed on-line April 8, 2005 at *http://www.bergconsultant.com/articles/live_systems/fear.htm*

3. Laura Laaman, "'Fear Factor' in Business: Cold Calls Have Chilling Effect," *Denver Business Journal*, March 25, 2005, p. 18.

4. Daniel Robin, "Three Faces of Fear in the Workplace," accessed on-line April 8, 2005, at *http://www.abetterworkplace.com.*

5. Chris Wenham, "Fear's Just Bad for Business," Dec. 18, 2001, accessed on-line April 8, 2005 at *http://www.disenchanted.com.*

6. Brian Norris, "Overcoming Negativity in the Workplace," accessed on-line April 8, 2005 at *http://www.briannorris.com.*

7. John Elder, "Increase Business Productivity with Anger Management Skills," accessed on-line April 8, 2005 at *http://angermanagementproviders.com.*

Additional Resources

Books

Bancroft, Lundy. *Why Does He Do That? Inside the Minds of Angry and Controlling Men*. Berkeley Publishing, 2003.

Bell, Arthur H. and Dayle M. Smith. *Winning with Difficult People 3e*. Barron's, 2004.

Bell, Arthur H. and Dayle M. Smith. *Management Communication*. Wiley, 1999.

Carter, Les. *The Anger Trap*.Wiley, 2003.

Dana, Daniel. *Conflict Resolution*. McGrawHill, 2000.

Davies, William. *Overcoming Anger and Irritability*. New York University Press, 2001.

Denise, Carolyn. *A Mother's Tongue*: *Overcoming Verbal Abuse*. Jawbone Publishing, 2004.

Elgin, Suzette Haden. *Genderspeak: Men, Women and the Gentle Art of Verbal Self-Defense*.Wiley, 1993.

Elgin, Suzette Haden. *You Can't Say That To Me! Stop ping the Pain of Verbal Abuse*. Wiley, 1995.

Ellis, Albert, et al. *The Secret of Overcoming Verbal Abuse*. Wilshire Book Company, 2000.

Evans, Patricia. The *Verbally Abusive Relationship: How to Recognize It and How to Respond, 2e.* Adams, 1996.

Evans, Patricia. *Verbal Abuse Survivors Speak Out.* Adams, 1993.

Glass, Lillian. *The Complete Idiot's guide to Verbal Self-Defense.* Alpha Books, 1999.

Grosshandler, Janet. *Coping with Verbal Abuse.* Rosen Publishing, 1989.

Harbin, Thomas. *Beyond Anger.* Marlowe & Company, 2000.

Hershorn, Michael. *60 Second Anger Management.* New Horizon, 2002.

Jarecke, George, et al. *Seeking Civility: Common Cour tesy and the Common Law.* Northeastern University Press, 2003.

Katz, Alice. *It's Not Personal! A Guide to Anger Man agement.* AJK Publishing, 1999.

Ketterman, Grace. *Verbal Abuse.* Servant Publications, 1992.

Lea, Speed. *Discover Your Conflict Management Style.* Alban Institute, 1998.

Mayer, Bernard. *The Dynamics of Conflict Resolution.* Jossey-Bass, 2000.

Ng, Sik, et al. *Power in Language: Verbal Communica tion and Social Influence.* Sage, 1993.

Schiraldi, G.R., et al. *The Anger Management Sourcebook.* McGraw-Hill, 2002.

Tafrate, R.C. *Anger Management.* Impact Publishers, 2002.

Thompson, George, et al. *Verbal Judo: the Gentle Art of Persuasion.* Quill, 2004.

Wellington, N.Z. *A Guide for Employers and Em ployees on Dealing with Violence at Work: Infor mation for Employers and Other People Who May Be Exposed to Physical Assault, Verbal Abuse, Threats or Intimidation.* Occupational Safety and Health Service, 1995.

Withers, William. *The Conflict Management Skills Workshop.* American Management Association, 2002.

Exploring Websites

The vast majority of Websites on abusive language, anger management, and conflict resolution offer a relatively small amount of general information followed by a list of services provided on a fee basis by a consultant, trainer, or psychologist. Among such websites are the following, no one of which is recommended over another but all of which bear investigation if you or your company seeks onsite or online assistance in developing and delivering employee training or personal work in the area of abusive language. No recommendation is expressed or implied for any particular for-fee organization.

www.accordsystems.com

www.andersonservices.com

www.angerclinic.com

www.angercoach.com

www.angercontrol.org

www.AngerManagementOnline.com

www.angermanagementtechniques.org

www.angermgmt.org

www.conflict911.com

www.sedona.com
www.selfhelpmp3.com
www.verbalabuse.com
www.verbalabuse.com
www.wordabuse.com
www.workplaceviolence911.com

Index

About the Author

Art Bell holds his Ph.D. in English from Harvard University and is Professor of Management Communication and Director of Communication Programs at the Masagung Graduate School of Management, University of San Francisco. He has previously held professorships in the Business Schools at Georgetown University and the University of Southern California.

In his MBA and Executive MBA classes, Art specializes in the development of short- and long-range communication architectures, missions, vision statements, and goals for established companies and entrepreneurial ventures. His background in communication, consumer behavior, and human motivation has helped him contribute as a lead consultant to strategic development projects and planning at Sun Microsystems, Cost Plus World Market, Apple Computer, Cushman-Wakefield, StarKist, Santa Fe Railway, Deutsche Telekom, the U.S. Navy, China Resources, Global Technologies, American Stores, Citicorp, TRW, Charles Schwab, the U.S. State Department, and many other organizations.

Art also specializes in managerial and executive coaching, particularly in the areas of conflict management (including verbal abuse situations), presentation skills, interviewing strategies, meeting leadership, gender communication, and intercultural communication. In the past two decades he has worked successfully with more than 2500 business people, ranging from CEOs to entry-level employees.

Art is the author of many books on current management topics, public speaking topics (especially speaker's nerves), language, and literature. Among his most recent books are *Phobias and How to Overcome Them* (Career Press, 2005), *Overcoming Anxiety, Panic, and Depression* (Career Press, 2001), *Winning with Truth in Business* (Pelican, forthcoming 2005), and *Management Communication 2e* (Wiley, forthcoming 2005). Other books include: *The Practicing Writer* (Houghton Mifflin, 1982), *Communication for Business and Management* (Scott Foresman, 1986), *Business Communication: Toward 2000* (South-Western, 1992), *The Complete Business Writer's Manual* (Prentice Hall, 1991), *Winning with Difficult People* (Barron's, 1997, 3rd ed. 2004), *Management Communication* (Wiley, 1999), *Communication for Managers* (South-Western, 1996), *Guide to Cliches* (Barron's, 1999), *Extraviewing: Innovative Ways to Hire the Best* (Irwin, 1992), *Learning Team Skills* (NTC, 1999), *Overcoming Anxiety, Panic, and Depression,* with James Gardner, M.D. (Career Press, 2001), *Great Jobs Abroad* (McGraw Hill 1999), *Intercultural Business* (Barron's, 2000), *International Careers* (Adams, 1995), *History of English Literature* (Barron's, 1999), *History of American Literature* (Barron's, 1999), *History of World Literature* (Barron's, 1999), *Mastering the Meeting Maze* (Addison Wesley, 1995), *Clear Technical Communication* (Harcourt, 1994), *Interviewing for Success* (Dow Jones, 1992), *Successful Technical and Business Communication* (South-Western, 1997), *Pocket Thesaurus* (Barron's, 1999, 2nd ed. 2003), *A Way with Words* (Asher Gallant, 1993), *The Speaker's Edge* (Asher Gallant, 1992), *The NTC Business*

Writer's Handbook (NTC/McGraw Hill, 1998), and *Writing Effective Letters and Memos* (Barron's, 1998, 2nd ed. 2003, 3rd ed. 2005). Other recent books include: *Measuring and Managing Knowledge* (McGraw-Hill, 2001), *Learning to Lead* (Prentice-Hall, 2002), *Developing Successful Teams* (Prentice Hall, 2002), *Motivating Yourself for Achievement* (Prentice Hall, 2002), *Successful Interviewing* (Prentice Hall, 2003), *Networking for Career Success* (Prentice Hall, 2003), *Speed Reading for Professionals*, (Barrons, 2005), and *Priority Management* (Prentice Hall, 2003).

Taken together, Art's books have been translated into fourteen languages. His articles on management topics have been published in more than 100 company and trade journals and magazines. In addition, Art is co-founder and senior partner in The One Week MBA , (on the internet at www.oneweekmba.com) a consulting firm specializing in the delivery of the latest MBA-level insights to managers and executives in concentrated on-site sessions.

On the personal side, Art is an aspiring (but not inspiring) jazz pianist, determined carpenter, book reviewer, and civic leader. He lives in Belvedere, CA with his wife, Dayle (also a business professor), and his two daughters. His son, Art Jr., is a diplomat for the U.S. State Department. Art can be contacted at 415-435-4245, email: bell.a@sbcglobal.net, mail: 16 Golden Gate Ave., Belvedere, CA 94920.